Value Added

HETTIE ASHWIN

Published by Slipperygrip 2022

Value Added
Copyright Hettie Ashwin

All rights reserved

PAPERBACK
ISBN:9782491490287
POCKET EDITION
ISBN: 9782491490294

www.linktr.ee/hettieashwin

chapter heading jpg.
Image by sentavio on Freepik

Books by Hettie Ashwin

<u>Humour</u>
<u>(10 terrific laugh out loud series)</u>
Literary Licence
The Reluctant Messiah
Mr Tripp buys a lifestyle
Barney's Test
The Truffle War
Fat Bits
Murder! Mayhem! and lesser cuts of meat.
I'd rather glue me nut sack to a bullet train
Nowhere near Anywhere
A Fate worse than death
Laughing Box set 1,2 & 3

<u>Humorous Memoir</u>
Boat to Baguette
Living it up in France

<u>Thriller</u>
The Crowing of the Beast

<u>Speculative fiction</u>
The Mask of Deceit
Pi - trilogy

<u>Short Stories</u>
After the Rains & other Stories
A shilling on the Bar

<u>Non fiction</u>
Productive Procrastination

<u>Novella series</u>
A strange kind of paradise 1-5
Box set.

A doctor can bury his
mistakes,
but an architect
can only advise his clients
to plant a vine

Frank Lloyd Wright

CHAPTER 1

The crassness of the form, the utter senselessness of the adornment seemed to rise up and slap him in the face. It hurt just to look at the thing, for there could be no other noun to describe the Monash House.

Jack swallowed—hard. His life depended on his answer. As a new kid on the block, fresh out of university with the ink still wet on his degree, he needed this job.

'Eh?' Jack was jogged out of his musing by the senior partner of Vuoto~Kopf Architects, a small Italian with a much bigger opinion of his talent and stature.

Mr Ricardo Vuoto smiled. A benevolent smile that Jack felt disarmingly friendly.

'I am saying it is something, no?'

'Errr,' Jack brought out a freshly laundered man size handkerchief and blew his nose rather than answer. *No,* thought Jack. It is something, but what, defied all he had learnt. Full of angles, rhomboids and Corinthian columns it looked like a child had thrown his Froebel blocks down in a tantrum. The moment was thankfully broken by one of Vuoto~Kopf's apprentices coming in with a small tray containing an espresso and a sticky bun. Mr Vuoto swooped on the offering and Jack's stomach gave a lurch. His brain kept his mouth firmly shut.

'Ah, from the God's, no?'

Jack nodded and wished for some manna from the heaven's himself. He'd only had a stale bagel for breakfast.

The apprentice winked at Jack and as Vuoto was occupied, mouthed the word, wonderment and left.

'It's a wonderment Sir.' Jack wasn't too dim witted not to grab a lifeline when it was thrown.

'You think?' Vuoto smiled.

'I do Sir.'

Ricardo Vuoto sipped and regarded the fresh face, the neatly parted hair and the eager visage of youth Jack displayed.

'Are you ...?'

'Oh yes definitely.' Jack jumped to conclusions like he was on a pogo stick.

He fiddled with his felt derby hat. It had cost him more than he was prepared to admit, but it was quality, the salesman said—last forever and bound to get you the job. He placed the derby on the seat next to him and picked off a bit of fluff as he listened with, what he hoped looked like, rapt attention.

'Here,' Vuoto spread his arms wide, 'here is the place we do the work of genius.'

'Genius,' Jack echoed.

'Si.' Vuoto strutted his 5'1 ½" to the window. He like this bit of an interview. His set piece as the apprentices call it. There was the bit about a team. The bit about being an individual. The mention of harmony and the description of the need for anger and passion. It was a performance worthy of an opera setting.

'Here,' Vuoto pointed to the skyline of the city beyond, 'here we make man to our own designs.'

'Absolutely.' Jack nodded and smiled. At this point in the interview he would have agreed to making man out of a doughnut stuffed with horse hair.

'So, there it is, no?'

'Er.'

Vuoto held out his hand, sticky with icing.

'Oh.' Jack took the proffered hand and that was that. He walked out of the office, his portfolio under his arm and wiped his fingers on his hanky.

'Welcome aboard,' Miss Faye Egan said with a lilting Irish accent. 'Mac.'

'Pardon?'

'They call me Mac.'

'Oh.' Jack looked at the young woman. He had heard they existed in the universe, but you can't dally with the opposite sex and get a first class degree, well Jack thought it unlikely anyway.

'So, Mac, how did you know?'

'What?'

'That I'd secured a position.'

'Oh that. You were in there,' she hoiked her head in the direction of the office, 'more than the allotted time.' Mac smiled. 'Here we make man to our own designs.' She held her finger aloft and then licked it miming Mr Ricardo Vuoto.

'Jack Renfrew,' he put his portfolio and hat down, shoved his handkerchief in his pocket and held out his hand.

'I know.' Mac smiled taking the offered hand.

'Of course.'

'Look Jack, a word of advice. Make yourself invisible until called upon.'

'Right.'

'You'll do just fine.'

'I hope so.'

'Abandon all hope ye who enter here.' Mac laughed.

'Er Mac?'

'Hmm?'

'About the wages. Mr Vuoto didn't exactly say.'

'Never does.' Mac looked at the red blinking light on her desk. 'Gotta go. Ciao.' She picked up her stenographer pad and with her pencil tucked behind her ear scooted towards Mr V's office. 'Monday. 8:45.' She threw the words in Jack's direction and closed the door. Jack stood for a moment and the door opened again,

'Sharp.' Mac shut the door.

Standing in the reception area of Vuoto~Kopf was a heady feeling. Being employed by the most prestigious firm in the city was euphoric. A smile began to creep over Jack's face which quickly turned into a wide grin.

'I have a job,' he said to the framed photographs on the wall. There was the Packwell Skyscraper, 1898, the Noonan Plaza, '99, The Postal Tower, '03, and the newly completed Louis Garrand Museum, 1909 all bearing the V~K signature.

'Hey.' A gangly young man sidled up to Jack.

'Yes.'

'Roman Ethan Thornton Huxley III.' He held out his hand. Jack took the hand with a firm grip.

'Nice to meet you Mr Huxley.'

'Oh, don't let the name fool you. The Huxleys don't have much to do these days.

'Right.'

'Practically the hoi polloi.' Roman laughed.

'Oh.'

'A house here and there. A boat or two. Nothing really.' Jack looked a little closer at the well-cut suit, the Italian shoes, the old school tie.'

'And you would be new blood?' Roman smiled and tipped his straw hat back on his head.

'Jack Renfrew. And you're the espresso guy.'

'Among other things if rumour is to be believed.'

'An apprentice?'

'That's right. Two years now.' Roman straightened his tie and rubbed the toe of his shoe on the back of his trousers, and together they looked at the Louis Garrand museum.

'I did that bit,' Roman pointed to the blockwork on the roof.

'Nice.'

'Yes isn't it.' They admired the line of blocks. 4' x 4' stacked in an orderly row.

'Thanks for the lifeline by the way.'

'Here we make man to our own designs.' Roman laughed.

'Wonderment.' Jack joined in.

'You hungry?'

'Hungry?' Jack thought of the $2.50 he had in his wallet. It was spoken for in rent, trolley fare and the rest of the week on small rations. He knew he had a piece of salami in his bedsit and half a packet of crackers. He had planned on seeing the woman at the end of the hall for a celebratory drink and perhaps a sandwich. Mrs Makowski was his surrogate mother figure, his friend, his confidant and a good source of wholesome Polish food.

'Yeah, want some lunch,' Roman asked.

'I guess.'

'Well, come with me.'

CB

The city buzzed with activity and an electricity of energy, drive and ambition. Jack never tired of walking the streets, seeing the buildings, the march of progress. 1910 was full of hope, purpose and prosperity. People jostled. People had places to go, things to do and at this time of day, lunch to procure.

'I know a place.' Roman looked over Jack's one good suit. 'Cheap too. Practically free.'

'Lead on.' Jack trotted behind Roman trying to keep pace with the fellow who had the legs of a pole vaulter.

'Here,' Roman pulled him into a laneway and they took a breath. The rubbish bins, the dank corners, the promise of rats didn't instil confidence of a ham sandwich and a cup of coffee.

Roman walked to a greasy door and rapped twice. He winked at Jack and whistled a tuneless tune.

The door opened, a brown paper bag was thrust into the air and the transaction took less than three seconds to complete.

Roman looked into the bag. 'From the Gods man was given the breath of life. Meatballs.'

They found a bench in a forlorn square of green that had seen much better days. It was dying a slow painful death, crowded by tall buildings, shade and automobile pollution. Jack scraped some chewing gum from his shoe and looked up.

'That's a Parker & Bedlow.'

'Correct.' Roman said. They admired the tall elegant building casting a shadow over the grass.

'Father bought in.'

'In what?'

'That.' Roman pointed to the skyscraper.

'Oh.' Jack thought on the money one might need to buy in. It made his head spin. He wondered why they were getting handouts at the back door if the Huxleys were, probably what the papers called, filthy rich.

As if reading his mind Roman continued,

'Father said I should make my way, so to speak. Silver spoon and that sort of thing.' Roman rolled his eyes and tipped his straw hat back on his head. 'I've got one year to go, then I will have done my penance as they say.'

'One year?'

'Three years ye shall toil. Then I get my allowance. A Huxley tradition. Make a man of the boy and then send him into the family business.' He laughed, an easy carefree laugh that was infectious. Of course mother slips a bit to me now and again.

Can't see the poor boy starve. Only she's gone abroad just now, hence my need for this,' he pointed to the bag of lunch. And with that Roman doled out meatballs into bread rolls and handed the gourmet meal over. 'Buon appetito.' It was surprisingly good.

'My girl works there. She's practically the head chef. She's Italian. Roman closed his eyes presumably dreaming of his Italian girl who was practically the head chef.

'You go to Newman South Shore University?'

'No.' Jack wiped his fingers on his hanky. 'Edelstein West.'

A whistle of surprise issued from Roman. 'Top marks to you.'

'Scholarship,' Jack said, trying to downplay the association with Edelstein West University and its reputation for elite excellence and astronomical fees.

'I did a stint in Paris. Mother was there and well ...' Roman waved his hand in the air.

'You don't mean the École des Beaux-Arts?' Jack's eyes popped at the thought of study in Paris with the masters.

'Just a lot of stuffed shirts if you ask me. Mother knew someone who knew someone and .... you know how it goes. C'est comme ça.'

'Pardon?'

'It is what it is.' Roman translated.

They ate in silence and looked at the skyscraper.

'I like you Jack.'

'Thanks. I like you too Roman.' Those words so often uttered in good faith would probably become one of those swords Damocles often dangled over one's head.

'And what of your heritage Mr Jack Renfrew? One of the East upper side Renfrews?'

'No' Jack shook his head. It wasn't easy to sum up his life in a few sentences. Orphaned at 10, and passed around to every relative until he ended at Uncle Fred and Aunt Mary's farm. A hard life, but a desire to 'do something' more than plough and spread muck.

'I come from farming.'

'Ah. Salt of the earth eh. Agriculture is the noblest of all alchemy. '

'Something like that,' Jack responded.

'Should you be back at work by now Roman?' Jack looked at his father's watch.

'Ol man Potato head won't be back 'till three.'

'Mr Kartoffelkopf?'

'Yeah. It literally means potato head. Go figure.' Roman gave a snort. 'My Alma Mata taught me something about language that comes in handy. And get this. Ol' Vuoto, he's Italian. My girl says his name means empty.

'Empty.'

'That's it. V~K Empty head.' Roman gave a guffaw and slapped Jack on the back. 'Funny eh?'

'I guess.' Jack looked at Roman's greasy fingers. He imagined the hand print over his one good suit. Mrs Makowski would know what to do.

'Smoke?'

'No thanks.'

'Sure?' Roman lit a cigarette and sat back. 'Yes siree Mr Jack Renfrew, we're going to get on just fine.'

Jack felt a tic develop in his eye.
 He wasn't so sure.

JACK RENFREW

Roman Ethan Thornton Huxley III

Home is where the heart is—the cross stitch motto had graced the chimney breast of the Brown farmhouse for as long as the house had a chimney. It had seen everything—and then some.

Now, the scene was set for a family gathering. The two words seem innocuous enough, but a Brown family gathering took a bit of organisation skill, a lot of cooking, and quite a bit of toing and froing to get the family of 17 all in the one place at the one time.

Bill Brown, a man who could pass as the quintessential Mid-West farmer, a man who had worn overalls most of his life, who knew the seasons by the smell of the earth and was, the salt of the earth, if the local newsletter in Brownsville was to be believed, now stood in the doorway of the porch and looked at the assortment of automobiles, motorbikes, bicycles and a couple of horses in the front yard. He scratched his balding head, shoved his gnarled hands in his pockets and frowned.

Bill called his wife, 'Enid, come look at this.'

'Enid, another earthy homespun type of person, wiped her hands on her apron and came to her husband's side. She put her arm around where his waist might be.

'What is it?'

'Can you believe all this.' He threw his hands wide over the array of vehicles. Bill was of the old school. A vehicle was a symbol of a disposable income, a sign that you were getting on in life. It looked like his family were doing alright.

'Oh Bill.' Enid gave him a shove on the shoulder.

'They're doin' alright.' The couple retreated to the kitchen and a hive of activity.

April, May and June set out the tea cups and saucers, while their husbands stood around like wall flowers. Hazel held a plate of scones while Holly held the dog plus baby Daisy. Rose busied herself by pulling napkins from the dresser. David, Dan and Douglas arranged chairs and Dunstan fetched the kettle from the wood stove.

'Settle down Edie,' Bill took his wife's elbow and placed her at the head of the table. The farmhouse kitchen fell silent.'

'Now I know,' Bill began, pushing his stomach into the small space between chair and table, 'Now I know we've been through it once, maybe twice, but it's time we settle this thing.' The 'thing' Bill alluded to was the farm. 'Mother and me, we're not gettin' any younger,' Bill held up his hand. 'No arguments.' The family watched as father warmed to his topic. They'd heard this preamble more than once. In fact they had been hearing it on and off for the last year or so, ever since Mother's stay in the hospital for her women's bits, as Bill was apt to describe to his neighbours.

Bill went on, 'I've got the block, the ol' Parson quarter acre. Mother and me want a house. Dougie and Beth will take the farm.' Bill patted Elizabeth's hand and the family looked at Douglas's very pregnant wife.

'Any day now,' she said and blushed.

Hazel chipped in, 'I'm having the loft... just until...' The family nodded in unison. No-one addressed the reason, it was too painful to relive being left at the altar.

'Watkins & Brown are drawing up papers,' Bill looked at Dan, the other half of Watkins & Brown. The Browns just about had the town of Brownsville sewn up. It wasn't named after the family, and in fact the first Mr William Brown senior only decided on a whim of fancy to lob up to Brownsville in 1822 because he fancied it would be a hoot. A bit of a joker was Will Brown Snr.

'With Dunstan off to University,' Bill gave a proud look at the baby of the family, 'Mother and me, well ...' Bill scratched the back of his neck, 'well we just...' Enid put a slice of lemon tart in front of Bill and he shrugged and took a bite.

Dan stood and recited the equal shares the family would receive. 'And with the sale of the north quarter mother and father should have enough.' Dan put the papers in his briefcase and the crowd fell upon scones, jam and cream, lashings of butter on fresh bread, cakes and jam tarts. More than enough to feed a family of 17 with another due any minute.

A gaggle of Browns. Aunts, Uncles, cousins and a dog or two.

It is quite easy to say, 'we want a house'. Four little words that pack a punch when you sit down and think about what a house might need, never mind what *you* want in the way of all modern appliances like electricity, running water, an indoor water closet and a bath, a big one if Bill has any say in the matter.

When the family had dispersed, the chores were done for the day, and it was that small moment of quiet in the old farmhouse, Bill and Enid brought out the catalogues and pulled two chairs up to the kitchen table. Under the old oil lamp they poured over modern living at affordable prices. If there is one thing that all farmers have in common, it is his love of a catalogue. A seed catalogue, a machinery catalogue, a build your own barn in an afternoon catalogue. They like 'em all. Bill went over the well-worn pages once again. He pointed out the fixtures and fittings for a bathroom. Enid nodded. All the man really wanted was his own bathroom for once. He'd shared with six daughters and four sons long enough. A man should be entitled to his own bathroom in his declining years. No more hair pins, blunt razors, or baby diapers.

Dunstan goes at the end of the summer,' Enid said looking at the pictures of kitchen ware.

'Douglas and Elizabeth will take over the house.' Bill added with a smile of satisfaction, thumbing the pages of soap dispensers.

'Holly is off to the West coast for her teaching position with baby Daisy and Ed.' Enid looked at the price of a new kettle. 'And Rose is boarding with Aunt Jane in the city while at the secretarial school for ladies,' Enid continued.

'And Hazel would soon be ....' Bill said and they looked up at the ceiling knowing Hazel was in the loft, probably trying to make the best of things and mend a broken heart.

'Do you think I should have one of these?' Bill pointed to a contraption, verified by Dr Malter, that would strengthen your spine while trying to pull it out of the top of your head as you bent over.

'Anything you want Bill.' Enid put a ring around an automatic egg timer with glow in the dark dial.

'The end of summer,' Bill said with a dreamy look. He would have his house by the end of summer. I mean, how hard can it be to build a house? A few bricks here, a pipe there and a roof and lickety split, a new bathroom with modern, hot and cold

chromatized taps at rock bottom bargain prices!
Damocles sharpened his sword.

CHAPTER 3

It is often the way that when you need to be
somewhere the Gods have other ideas. The Gods –
or the Municipal Trolley Company were in cahoots
with the Gods it seemed as the passengers sweated
it out waiting for some movement

Jack leaned over from the standing room only
aisle to look out of the window and caught his
coat button on a rather large floral and feather
arrangement on a hat. The young woman tilted
her head and Jack could do nothing but mirror the
action while trying to untangle himself.

'Excuse me,' he tapped the woman on the
shoulder. She looked up and gave her hat a tug in
the opposite direction while ignoring his overture.

'Miss.' He tugged at his button and it popped
off and added itself to the floral arrangement more
suited to a botanical garden.

'Oh damnation.'

'I beg your pardon young man,' a fellow in a

bowler hat glowered.

Not only would he be late for his first day, he couldn't button his suit coat.

The rumours of a horse, an accident, a woman under the wheels, a dray overturned, an escaping criminal and a dog on the road circulated in the trolley. Jack watched the minutes tick by. There was nothing for it. He jumped off and began to walk. Pedestrians have no sense of direction. They dither, stroll, bump and shove and generally behave like chickens.

'Excuse me, sorry, pardon,' he pushed and elbowed his way down the main thoroughfare. He pressed on trying to keep his coat from flapping, his hat on, not squash his lunch and remain calm. The minutes ticked by as his every effort was thwarted by people.

The Boulder Insurance Building was just ahead, V & K on the fourth floor. Jack looked up and was pushed and hustled into the traffic. He watched his lunch get squashed by an automobile, his hat about to receive the same fate.

'Hey,' he shouted.

'Watch it,' the woman driver shouted back as she accelerated away.

'Thought it was you,' Roman took Jack by the elbow and ushered him to the other side of the street.

'Roman.'

'In person.'

'Did you see that. That dang woman nearly ran me down.'

'I did. Shocking what these women get up to these days, isn't it.' Roman smirked.

Jack looked at his watch. He had about three minutes up his sleeve. 'I need to...'

'Don't worry. We have plenty of time.' Roman dusted off Jack's hat and handed it to him. 'I usually drive, but as it was such a pleasant day I thought I'd walk.'

Jack was inclined to run. 'I really think I should be there,' he pointed to the Boulder Insurance Building.

'Oh. Right.' Huxley made a face. 'If you must.'

'I must.' Jack sprinted and arrived via the stairs with one minute to spare.

The fourth floor was an airy, lofty place. It contained the offices of the partners, a board room and a partitioned area for the head draftsman, Mr Stanley Cohan.

Mac looked at the large clock on the wall and then at Jack.

'Sorry. An accident on Main.'

'Mr Otto Kartoffelkopf likes his workers to be prompt.' Mac straightened Jack's tie and took his hat. 'Did you run all the way?' she looked at his coat.

All Jack could do was grin sheepishly and shrug his shoulders.

'Mr Kartoffelkopf would like to see you. In there,' Mac pointed to a solid door with the name in gold. 'He won't bite, but he can't abide idiots. Don't give him the idea you're an idiot.'

'Right.'

'And...'

'Yes?'

'He thinks he's surrounded by idiots.' Jack

nodded and followed Mac into the lion's den.

Mr K's reputation for innovation, excellence and an unnerving ability to go over budget was known far and wide. He was, he would remind you, schooled in Europe. He liked to think of himself as European and that he was practically related to the Bauhaus gang, and on first name terms with those of the arts and craft movement. As far as Mr K was concerned he was architectural royalty. What some said in private was another matter.

Mr Otto Kartoffelkopf was a short, rotund, Bratwurst. He was Teutonic down to his Weiner schnitzel if you asked, but his lineage was pure American on his mother's side. His father had instilled a Teutonic flavour to his son and it had stuck. His accent was somewhere between New York and the old country and came out sounding like he was perpetually rolling his eyes, surrounded by idiots. That he had a florid and sometimes incomprehensible vocabulary only added to the illusion.

'Sit.'

Jack sat.

'You will know we only do the best work here, ja?' Mr K polished his spectacles.

Jack nodded.

'We only have one motto. Better than Best.' The spectacles were placed on his nose.

'Definitely Sir.' Jack tried to look eager and intelligent at the same time. It was a fine line between looking simple and an idiot.

'You will work ja. You will throw out everything you know and start again.' The spectacles were given another polish. 'I am ...' And here Mr K threw himself into describing his schooling in Europe etc etc. Jack listened, but after the fifth minute his concentration waned and his gaze wandered to the view from the window.

'Universities have an aberrant incapacity to prepare students for the real world of architectural practice, ja.' Mr K warmed to his pet subject, one of many you might discover, if you had to spend any time with him. He continued, 'a fantasy world of incompetent professors who thrive on personality cults, and don't teach anything of the hard realities of life.' Mr K squinted at Jack.

Jack looked at the man and formed a picture of a potato. Mr K waffled on a bit more and ended with, '...from you, ja?'

Jack snapped back to the present with, 'I will?'

'Yes, we will build the man to our own designs, ja?' Mr K thumped the desk. Jack jumped, the only question was, how high.

'Follow me,' Mac led Jack down the stairs to the basement. Here it didn't look so inviting, spacious and grand.

'Jenkin used to sit over there,' Mac pointed to a table and stool in the corner. She led him to a coat rack. 'Jenkin's dust coat,' she pointed to the buff colour coat. 'If Mr V or Mr K venture down here, do the buttons up.' She looked at Jack's suit coat.

'Right.'

'Jenkins took up his 165 acres from the

Government and went out west. A farmer.'

There was an audible snort from the fellow draftsmen. Jack knew just what they meant. He shuddered at the thought of farming and shrugged on Jenkin's coat, hung his hat on Jenkins peg and pulled on Jenkin's sleeve garters. Mac looked at him.

'Here are three pencils. They will be deducted.'

It was a phrase all the apprentices grew to hate.

Sitting in the corner Jack looked at his drafting table. Jenkins was obviously a doodler. He tried to decipher some of the more elaborate drawings. He put his pencils on the table, then pocketed two. He looked at his finger nails, then at his pencil. All he could hear was the sound of set squares moving across paper, the scratch of pen and ink, and a heavy breather somewhere.

'Oh, here already Renfrew.' Huxley breezed in and after depositing his coat, putting his hat on the peg and donning his dust coat he took up his stool.

The other young men were diligent in their labours. No-one spoke. Jack spied the water jug and fetched a drink. The morning wore on, although it might have been afternoon—it was hard to tell in the dungeon with no windows.

'Er.' Jack stood at the table of his nearest neighbour.

'Hmmm?'

'Jack Renfrew.' He held out his hand.

'Elliott Swindon.' Elliott squinted up at Jack then looked at his drawing, back at Jack then picked up his pencil.

'Mr Clarence Putney,' the heavy breather leaned

in and held out his hand.

'Jack Renfrew.'

'Look, we are a bit busy. V & K are behind.'

There was a snort of derision from the four in the room.

'Can I be of any help?'

'The thing is, we'd quite like a bit of help, but you see, we get paid on our signature, and well, it's like this ...'

'What ol' pal Putney is trying to say,' Huxley chimed in, 'is that the allotted kitty of money from Mr Monash's house to our humble department will be divided between us. You can see the problem can't you dear Jack.'

'Oh, yes absolutely.' Putney and Swindon went back to work.

'Gilbert Steinbeck,' the tall pimply youth held out his hand.

'Nice to meet you.'

'If you are any good at flower pots, I could use a hand. Never any good at trees and flower pots. I could spot you lunch if that's alright?'

'Anything to be of assistance.' Jack looked over the drawing of the front elevation.

'Here, here and about a dozen others.' Gilbert waved his hand over the line drawing and then gave it to Jack. 'I can ink them, if you can draw them. Mr K likes a bit of realism.

'Realism.'

'Yes, that's right.'

An urn of flowers might not give you a living wage, but a salami sandwich would keep you alive.

'What is this? Mr Kartoffelkopf looked at the

drawing of the Monash residence as the light faded in his office. The clock chimed 7 o'clock as the five draftsmen stood and hoped they could go home.

'Flowers?' Gilbert squeaked a reply.

'Nasturtiums,' Jack added, then pointed to an urn on a plinth, 'delphiniums.' Mr K frowned and studied Jack's face.

'Who are you?'

'Mr Jack Renfrew sir.'

'And you did this,' Mr K pointed to the riot of spring flowers and shrubs.

'Yes sir.'

Steinbeck, Huxley, Putney and Swindon took a step back. They had heard that tone of voice before. The blast from the furnace of Mr K's indignation might singe one's eyebrows if one stood too close.

The clock chimed the quarter hour. The Monash house might have been spectacular in design, but it was spectacularly overdue. Mr Monash was waiting on the drawings, his bank was waiting on the drawings, his wife, well she had a few things to say about the drawings.

Mr K came in close. He pulled off his spectacles and gave them a polish. He replaced them and came in closer.

'Pelargoniums.'

'You don't say.' Mr K looked up at Jack.

'Yes.' Jack then pointed to a shrub. 'Hydrangea.'

'Ah.' Mr K stood up. 'It is done, ja.'

There was a collective sigh as the men began to breathe.

'Of course we always give something to the ladies.'

'Yes sir.'

'I remember ....' and Steinbeck, Huxley, Putney, Swindon and Renfrew had to wait until Mr K had climbed another mountain, picked another bunch of Edelweiss, and set a record for aggrandisement before they could go home.

It was only as he was getting into bed that Jack wondered how much a living wage might be and when he was likely to receive it to start living.

CHAPTER 4

Hazel and Rose Brown alighted from the train and hauled their carpet bags down to the platform. The porter hovered, but if he was angling for a tip, he was mistaken. The Brown girls were of the no-nonsense kind who could manage very well, thank you very much. They were of the type that might shoe an horse, give birth and whip up a batch of muffins before you had time to tie your boot lace.

'Oh, there she is,' Rose waved at their Aunt Jane, another salt of the earth type who might grind six inch nails in her sleep.

'Girls, girls,' Aunt Jane shoved past the crowd and threw her arms wide. 'Oh, let me look at you.' She made them twirl. 'Browns, no doubt about it.' The Browns were blessed with freckles and hazel eyes.

'You'll never guess.' Aunt Jane pushed her hat down and began to lead the girls away.

'Our bags.' Hazel picked up the bags and

followed along.

'I've just purchased an automobile. Slickest thing you ever saw.' Aunt Jane shoved a man out of the way. 'Goes like the wind.'

'Really?'

'A Ford, Model T motor buggy. Mr Ford said I could have any colour as long as it's black.' Aunt Jane hooted with pleasure. 'Good ol' American know how. I've called her Nike, Goddess of speed.'

They stood and admired the vehicle. It was in the process of getting some attention from a police officer.

'Here, what's this?' Aunt Jane fronted the officer.

'This yours Madam?'

'It is.'

'Well you can't stop here.'

'I'm just leaving.' Aunt Jane turned to her nieces. 'Hop in.' She repositioned her hat, and then proceeded to crank the engine over. These women who are brought up on a farm would give an arm wrestler a run for his money.

Aunt Jane in her heyday.

Purchasing a motor buggy and driving said buggy are two different things. Mrs Osborne Parker, widowed, nee Brown, might have been the salt of the earth, but she still had a few things to learn about the safe and careful operation of an automobile.

'Hang onto your hats girls,' Aunt Jane, let go of the brake, shoved the vehicle into forward motion and they jerked their way into the traffic. The gears crunched and ground as Aunt Jane mangled the clutch operation.

'Aunt,' Hazel yelled over the engine, 'Douglas taught me how to drive. I could help if you like.'

The Ford was pulled over to the chagrin of the other road users and a fair bit of honking, then Hazel positioned herself in the driver's seat.

'It's quite simple really,' Hazel extended her arm, waved her hand around and pulled into the traffic.

'There,' Aunt Jane pointed to a three story town house and Hazel brought the Model T to a halt.

'Marvellous, simply marvellous.' Aunt Jane slapped her pride and joy.

'It was this,' she patted her Model T, 'or indoor plumbing. You can't go to town in a bathtub.'

The town house was full of curios from Mr Parker's explorations. Rose and Hazel looked over the elephant umbrella stand to the stuffed moose head on the wall acting as a coat rack.

'Don't stand on ceremony, come in, come in.' Aunt Jane threw her driving coat on the moose and called for her housekeeper, maid, confidant and friend, 'Clarissa, tea I think.'

Eventually, the conversation over tea came to the painful events of the last month and Hazel's well-being.

'Well, you must get out my girl. Back on the horse as they say. I can introduce you to my set. A lively bunch.'

Hazel inwardly winced. Aunt Jane's set were probably old, played cards and gossiped incessantly.

'Oh, I'll be alright,' she sipped her tea.

'Tosh. You need stimulation my girl.'

'I really think ...'

'Hazel Euphemia Brown. If there is one thing your Aunt knows about, it is stimulation. Good for the mind and body. I attended a lecture by Miss Ludwick and she advised us that women need stimulation to fulfill our destiny.'

'Our destiny?'

'I have a wonderful idea.' Aunt Jane slapped her thigh. 'You can start by giving me driving lessons in Nike.'

'I can't stay Aunt Jane.'

'What? Nonsense. You will stay with me. I'll see to it you forget what's-his-name.'

'I really need to get back. I only came to give Rose company on the train. Mother didn't want her to come alone.'

'Well I insist. I will write a letter this instant. Bill will understand. You will be of valuable assistance to your Aunt Jane, and that is that.'

Hazel looked at Rose and shrugged her shoulders.

'You might get a job,' Rose said, tucking into

another sandwich.

'A job.'

It sounded like a good idea, although there might not be much call in the city for a farm girl who could throw a hay bale, shoe a horse, and mend a fence.

Miss Hazel Brown in her natural habitat

'I know. I'll send a telegram.' Aunt Jane said.

'Really?' Hazel and Rose exclaimed together.

'Mr Parker was fond of 'em. He would say, Jane, send a wire.' Aunt Jane stood up, 'Clarissa,' she called.

'Oh, let me Aunt Jane. I can do it. I'll take Nike if I may?'

'Excellent idea Hazel.'

A dispatch was authored, the money counted and Hazel scooted out the door.

A Ford Model T, 1910.

The Model T was a splendid example of American engineering. Hazel relished the freedom it provided. She was relishing that freedom when turning a corner a hat blew straight into her face and only with quick thinking did she avoid an accident with a horse and buggy.

'Hey!' Jack ran after the automobile, 'my hat.' After a block and a half, Hazel came to a halt in front of the Telegraph office and collected her purse when Jack caught up.

'You have my hat,' he harangued Hazel and tried to peer into the vehicle.

'Really?'

'Yes Miss. You have my hat.'

Hazel looked at the derby which had rolled to the footwell. 'I don't think so sir.'

'I beg your pardon?'

'I don't have your hat. Now if you would kindly take your arm off my automobile I have important business to attend to.' Hazel made her way to the telegraph office with a smirk on her face.

Jack stood back, his ire rising. 'Damnation.' Then he took matters into his own hands. Scouting around for witnesses and on seeing none, he opened the driver side door and climbed in to look for his hat.

'Ah, ha!' Jack was in the act of bending down when Hazel returned.

'Excuse me,' she poked Jack's back with a gloved hand.

'Eh?' Jack sat up.

'I think you will find you are sitting in my automobile without my permission.'

'And I think you will find that you stole my hat.'

'Are you quite sure of your facts sir?'

'I am Miss.'

Hazel smiled. 'I hear practical jokes are all the rage this season.'

'And I hear theft has always been in season.' Jack began to exit the Ford. He stopped and calculated the expense, plus the young attractive women who didn't quite fit the filthy rich set.

'Is this your vehicle?' he asked with a steely glare.

'Not that it is any of your business sir, but it belongs to my Aunt.

'Ah.' Law abiding people often say 'ah' when they jump to conclusions. Jack was on his pogo stick again.

'Ah to you. Now, if you would be so kind,' Hazel stepped back so Jack could open the door.

'How do I know you didn't thieve it?'

'What?'

'You're a thief. How do I know you are telling the truth?'

'Don't be ridiculous.'

'I could call the police. This sort of thing happens you know.' The combatants eyed one another.

'Get in.' Hazel pointed to the passenger seat. 'I will prove my claim.'

Jack looked at his watch. He was sent out to check on the Louis Garrand's leaking roof and its progress. He was supposed to be working. Mr K's words echoed in his thoughts.

'Builders are not to be trusted. Ja. They don't know your face. Go and see what they are doing and then come and tell me. Ja.' Spying didn't take long, and so Jack walked a block or two to admire the Russell Mutual Assurance Building. It stood on a corner with a permanent scowl as if to say 'how dare you'. It was christened 'humbug' by the city dwellers after another with a permanent scowl— Scrooge of Charles Dicken's fame. It also had the distinction of funnelling wind from both sides— enough wind to take a man's hat off.

'Need to be somewhere?'

'Well, yes. As a matter of fact I do.' Jack said.

'But first my reputation must be reinstated. Hazel handed the cranking handle to Jack.

'Hang onto your hat,' Hazel laughed.

'In the circumstances Miss I decline to find that funny.' Jack smiled and with a wave of Hazel's hand they pulled out into mid-town traffic.

'Mr Jack Renfrew.'

'Miss Hazel Brown,' The introductions were

made over an intersection, Hazel extending her hand.

'Miss.' Jack gave a cursory handshake. Hazel reapplied her efforts to driving.

'You drive remarkably well.'

'Oh?' Hazel kept her eyes on the road. 'For a woman you mean?' She narrowed her eyes and set her jaw.

'No, I just meant, well, sort of...well.'

'Mr Renfrew. The first rule of holes. Stop digging.'

The remainder of the trip was in silence, Jack afraid to blot his copy book even more with this young strong-headed woman.

They turned a corner and came to a stop.

'My aunt's residence. My aunt's Ford.'

There was a twitch of the curtains as Aunt Jane exclaimed to Clarissa,

That girl doesn't waste any time. She's got a man already.'

'Come on.' Hazel led Jack to the front steps.

'Really Miss Brown, I don't think you are a thief.' Jack looked at his watch.

'I wouldn't want you to get the wrong impression Mr Renfrew.' She took to the steps.

'Look, I should just go.'

'Mr Renfrew, this way,' Hazel was about to knock when the door opened. She turned to Jack, 'My aunt. Mrs Osborne Parker. Aunt Jane, Mr Jack Renfrew.'

'Pleasure.' Aunt Jane stood back to let the couple inside.

'Aunt, this gentleman was under the impression I stole that,' Hazel pointed to the Ford. He presumes

I'm a thief.'

'Oh my goodness.'

'Mrs Parker, I think it is a rather large misunderstanding.' Jack blushed and shuffled his feet

'A misunderstanding?'

'A rather large one.'

Aunt Jane looked from Hazel to Jack and back again. 'Tea Mr Renfrew?'

If Aunt Jane had a curriculum vitae, top of the list would be her uncanny knack of wheedling information from the unsuspecting. Mr Parker might have been an explorer and adventurer—discovering new and exciting worlds, but he couldn't hold a candle to his wife when it came to getting the who, what, when, where and why.

In the course of scones and tea Jack was grilled, flattered, and pumped like a Texas oil well.

'Oh, I'd love a new house. I've always fancied a museum of sorts for all this,' Aunt Jane waved her arms to take in the musty library, the shelves of exotic curios, the collection of Japanese pottery and the odd shrunken head.

'Vuoto & Kartoffelkopf are world renowned, Mrs Parker.' Jack peered at the shrunken head.

'Really?'

'Oh yes.' There was something charming about the boy with his eagre face, his innocence and his good manners.

'I have an idea of sorts.' Aunt Jane said.

'I could arrange an appointment if you would give me your card Mrs Parker.'

'My boy, I would be delighted.'

And that was how, instead of getting the sack for tardiness, Jack was promoted from urns to finials—architectural ornamental terminations—or to the more uneducated, those delicate fiddly bits on top.

And to top it off (*author note*, I just had to put that in) that was how Jack found himself in the lucky position of escorting Miss Brown to the new Louis Garrand Museum on a Sunday afternoon.

ꝏ

Whatever the discipline, the enthusiast becomes an authority when they have a captive audience. Jack guided Miss Brown up the steps and pointed out the various bits of the museum.

'These are the Venetian influenced stairs,' he said.

'This is an arch with a key stone,' he pointed.

'This is a door.'

One never quite knows what the casual observer's education standard on the topic might be, but the opportunity to be condescending is almost limitless.

Hazel took it all in her stride as she was 'educated'.

'And this would be a window,' she said and waited, a smirk developing behind her gloved hand.

'Ah, right.'

'I appreciate it Mr Renfrew, really I do.'

'It's Jack.'

'Hazel.' They shook hands in a friendly truce.

Their gaze wandered to the inscription over the

inner portal archway cut deep into the pink granite in a font more suited to a greeting card from a favourite Aunt than a pithy quote from antiquity.

FABRUM ESSE SUAE QUEMQUE FORUNAE
Appuis Caecus.

'What does it mean?'

'Each man the architect of his own fate.'

'What about women?'

Jack had only ever known strong independent women. It never occurred to him that women were not his equal.

'Of course. Man, here is used in the general sense. Mankind.' It came out sounding like a lecture to a recalcitrant student.

He tried to save the moment.

'Your aunt is quite something isn't she.'

'Yes, she is.' Hazel said with a bit of derision.

'What I mean is she's lively.'

'Yes.' Hazel could see the man was trying his best. She let him off the hook. 'She's always been game.'

'And your Uncle, Mr Parker?'

'Dead I'm afraid.'

'Oh, I am sorry to hear that.'

'Not as sorry as he was,' Hazel laughed and began the story of Mr Osborne Parker, adventurer, explorer and 'a prolific collector of things.'

'Things?'

'From around the world. You must have seen the 'things' in the library?'

'Ah. Things.' Jack remembered the shrunken head.

'And your aunt, was she his companion through

thick and thin?'

'Some of the time. Then, she finally had enough of the thick and thin. Uncle would travel and aunt would take charge of the boxes that kept coming home.'

Jack listened with rapt attention. It all sounded like something one read about in a book.

They made their way to an exhibition of native spears and shields.

'Is that your uncle?'

~Osborne Parker—last know artefact.

The artefact in question a spear, pulled out of his back and brought home as a museum piece.

'Aunt Jane says Uncle Osborne was a martyr to his collection.'

They looked at the spear.

'Must have been devilishly painful.'

'A bit more painful than philately.'

They settled down with a pot of tea for two and a stale fruit scone each.

'You know my mother and father want a new house.' Hazel looked at the tall columns of the tea room. 'Nothing too grand.'

'Hmm.'

'We have a farm.'

'Hmmm.'

'Father wants something modern, nice.'

'Nice.' Jack gazed at Hazel.

'Does your firm do that sort of thing, build small houses I mean?'

'Oh yes.' Jack nodded. 'We do.'

'Do you think if mother and father came to your

office, they might get what they want?'

'Hmm.'

'Are you listening to me Jack?'

'What? Yes. Absolutely.'

'Could you arrange it?'

'Anything.' Jack ate his scone. He might have been eating a classic stone ball finial as his mind wandered to a place where all young men's minds wander when they find the opposite sex inhabit their world.

For the readers information, the scone might well have been a stone ball, they weren't a best seller and three days old.

CHAPTER 5

For a top shelf practice like V & K they preferred not to tout for business. Clients—some well-heeled, would beat a path to their door in the hope of getting a house, a building or even a monument in death that would increase in value as the years ticked by, just by dint of association. Although, having a mausoleum that was prime real estate rarely benefited the occupant.

'One day our light fittings will be worth their weight in gold no!' Mr V was the financial wizard of the outfit with a hankering for the finer things of life—which necessitated some creative accounting that Houdini might have been proud. Now you see it, now you don't.

V & K were synonymous with the 'must have' of the season and one simply must have a mausoleum, summer cottage or dog kennel designed by Mr V or Mr K.

Architects, whether a must have item or not, are,

when it comes down to brass tacks, just like any other tradesmen. No-one can say with any certainty where the next commission might be coming from, or if it will come at all. So, in the time honoured tradition of tradesmen, they invariably say 'yes', 'naturally', and 'of course', to any and all work that comes their way, calling it 'something to fall back on.' It also invariably plays havoc with work schedules.

V & K had four houses on the drawing boards, one opera House that was almost in the bag, a holiday home that was stalled because of weather, and the Monash house.

The Monash house was spread across the apprentice's tables. Mrs. Monash had decided she needed a solarium on the north side of the house. The logic of putting a solarium on the dark side of the moon wasn't lost on the apprentices. But it meant an extra few days' work, which meant a bit more in the pocket at the end of the month. Jack worked on the frieze across the top depicting the rays of the sun shining down benevolently. He hoped some of Mr. Monash's benevolence might swing his way. Things were getting grim, and Mrs. Makowski was going to her sisters for a week.'

'Roman,' Jack said, 'when are we likely to get paid?'

'Ah, the root of all evil.' Roman said putting his pencil down.

'Yes. That's the stuff.'

'End of the month. Mr. V comes down, bestows his blessings in small envelopes.

'He says we are too young to appreciate what

money can provide.' Swindon chimed in.

'That's why we don't get much.' Steinbeck added.

'And don't open it until he's gone. He thinks of it as charity.' Putney gave a snort.

'Right.'

Jack thought he might need some charity, if he didn't get enough to pay his rent. Starving to death was a mere trifle in comparison to being on the street.

His stomach gave a gurgle and he stopped work and thought on the conversation he'd just had with Mac. After giving her Mrs Parker's card and the promise of a house for the Brown's he thought of more money for the practice, and the theory of trickle-down economics.

Mac had looked at him 'Didn't I say invisible?'

'Ah, well ...' Jack shrugged his shoulders and looked sheepish.

'What are you doing? Running people down to sign them up?'

'No. Nothing like that.'

'Well whatever it is you do, stop it.' Mac shook her head. 'We are up to here,' she waved her hand over her head, 'with projects.'

'But isn't that a good thing?' Jack frowned. Mac looked at the head draftsman in his little office. Mr Cohan was almost bent double over his table. He didn't look happy.

'Mr K dreams up the concept.' Mac took a breath. 'Mr V looks at it, refines it, tries to cost it. Do you follow me?'

'Yes, so far so good,' Jack said and sat down.

'Mr K shouts about art. He shouts about the

three F's. Form follows function at every available opportunity as though he invented them. The marriage of genius with the construction of art. He calls everyone a philistine and an idiot. Art has no price.' Mac thumped the desk. 'You'll hear that a lot.'

'Hmmmm.'

'And then Mr V has another go. Still with me?'

'Yes.'

'Then ol' misery guts in there,' Mac pointed to Mr Cohan, 'draws the thing of genius.'

'Right.' Jack looked at the head draftsman and wondered if he was ever happy.

'Then the owner sets down how much he has to spend. More work, more genius sacrificed to filthy lucre,' Mac said.

'Filthy lucre?'

'Money Mr Renfrew. Then and only then do the plans go down to you to render something that a bank can understand, a lawyer can look at, a wife can admire and a man who will probably go into hock to convince himself that although a deep and lasting wound he won't die building his dream house, can call worthwhile.' Mac sat back and picked up her pencil.

'But are they happy?' Jack asked.

'Pfffft.'

CHAPTER 6

Bill Brown was happy. He and Enid stood on the platform with their bags and watched Hazel wend her way through the people to greet them. She waved. They waved back and then there were hugs, kisses, and the general business of bags, news, gossip and fending off porters who were fishing for a tip. Bill and Enid picked up their bags and followed their daughter through the throng of city life.

'What's this?' Bill eyed the Model T.

'Aunt Jane's new automobile. It's nicknamed Nike—Goddess of speed.'

'Oh my giddy aunt.' Enid looked at the plush seats. 'Bit different to the farm, eh Bill,' Enid jabbed her husband in the ribs.

'Just a bit.' Bill tipped his hat back on his head and whistled. Then he walked around the Model T. 'Hot dog!'

'Bill.' Enid gave him a dig in the ribs.

Bill wasn't a complete yokel in the city. He had read the catalogues, he knew what was on offer in the metropolis. From Burrow's automatic soap dispensers to Mr McCreedy's porcelain emporium he knew his chromatic taps from his brass couplings.

'Move it along,' A policeman poked Bill with his baton.

'Eh?'

'I said move it.'

'Come on father. Aunt Jane is waiting.'

'That's my daughter.' Bill tipped his hat to the policeman. 'She's driving me to my sister's place. We're going to engage an architect to build a house.'

Bill was quite adept at talking the hind leg off a donkey. Country folk are friendly folk. Always ready for a chinwag.

The policeman nodded. 'You just come from the country then?'

'That's right. Came on the 7:10 from Brownsville. Bill Brown.' He held out his hand. The policeman shook it.

'Not that Brownsville is my town, no. It is one of those co-incidences you hear about. My grandfather....' and Bill might have told the whole Brown family history if Enid hadn't poked him in the ribs. Marriage is like that. Little signs of affection. A sort of secret language to tell you when to shut up.

'Well, good luck to you farmer Brown.' The policeman tipped his hat.

Hazel gave the Ford a crank and rolled down her sleeve.

'I'm going to give Aunt Jane driving lessons,' she said as she waved her hand about and merged into the ever increasing traffic.

'Oh, my giddy aunt.'

More hugs, more kisses and eventually the Browns got beyond the front door of the Parker residence and into the library.

Clarissa brought in tea and cake and the family settled in.

'Good train ride down?'

'Yes.'

'Rose is at college.' Hazel said. She'll be back at three.

'Hazel is giving me driving lessons.' Aunt Jane took a bit of cake.

'Nice weather.' Enid sipped her tea.

Bill ate in silence.

When you've been corresponding regularly for years, there really isn't much to say. It's all been said.

'I made an appointment with the architect.' Hazel offered a slice of cake to her father.

'Ah.' Bill said.

'The day after tomorrow.'

'That would be Wednesday.'

'Yes.' Hazel fiddled with her tea cup.

What to do with your parents for one day in the city was a conundrum. They were not the types to traipse about the place looking at monuments. She couldn't see them walking through a museum and marvelling at an inscription about man and his fate. Mother might enjoy the shopping emporiums, but father would make a face.

'Um, did you have something to do tomorrow?'

Hazel hoped they wanted to rest, relax and keep Aunt Jane occupied.

'Well I'm glad you asked.' Bill brought out a little book with an even smaller pencil. 'I thought I might take a look at McCreedy's Porcelain Emporium.

'Right.'

'And then I would like to visit Burrows, Avery's, Warners and White.' Bill closed his little book.

'If we have time, I'd like to see Mrs Prestons home furnishings and drapery.' Enid brought out a catalogue and pointed to the drapery. 'Corner of Wickam and Southshore.'

'Right.' Hazel looked at Aunt Jane.

'Of course you can my dear.' Hazel was beginning to love that automobile as if it were her own.

A day admiring indoor plumbing and curtain fittings might not be a young woman's idea of a good time, but for two country folk, it was stimulating and educational. Reading catalogues puts ideas in one's head—seeing the item, be it a modern automated sock stretcher or Dr Wrights patented liver and spleen purifier—well, it was just about as up-to-the-minute as you could get.

Hazel chauffeured her parents around the city, which was the saving grace of the day. Her driving was improving every minute.

'I am to give Aunt Jane her lesson this afternoon. Do you think we could go home now?'

Bill and Enid looked over their booty of pamphlets, advertisements and free samples.

'Yep. That's about it, isn't it mother?'

'Oh yes.' Enid sat back to enjoy the ride to Aunt Janes.

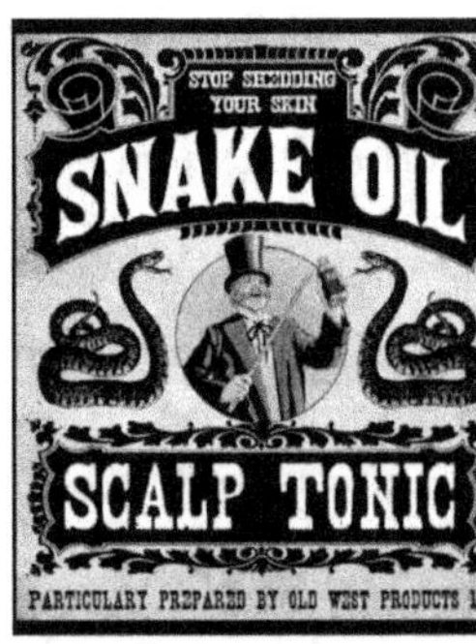

Some people have the patience of Job, others not so much. Aunt Jane was impulsive, impatient and immune to tooting of horns, exclamations of surprise and the odd word of encouragement from other road uses, ie 'Get off the road' and 'watch it lady!'

Hazel gritted her teeth and went through the procedure for a left turn once again as they went around the block for the fifth time.

'I really think you're getting better Aunt Jane.'

'Ya think.'

'Oh, yes....slow....slow....look to your right and hand signal and turn.' They drove down the boulevard in a slow stately fashion. 'Over there Aunt.' They came to a stop with a neck snap of the gears as Aunt Jane tried to co-ordinate the clutch, the brake and the hand signal.

'Marvellous, simply marvellous.' Aunt Jane brought out a hip flask. 'For my nerves.' Hazel took the flask and put it in her pocket.

'Let's get home first shall we.'

Hazel rubbed the back of her neck as Clarissa poured the afternoon tea for the family.

'I should like another lesson Hazel. I feel with your instruction I could drive to Monte Carlo.'

'Well Mrs Alice Ramsey went across our continent in her automobile, so Monte Carlo it is.' Hazel laughed.

'I saw her off you know. Went to the city and waved.' Aunt Jane poured her tea. An amazing woman, and a wonderful achievement. To think she went all that way driving herself and her companions. I read all about it in the gazette. What a feat, so I feel quite capable. Monte Carlo it is.'

'Oh Aunt Jane.' Hazel gave her head a twist as her neck crackled and snapped.

'You are a marvel of saintly patience.' Aunt Jane added.

'Isn't she.' Enid said taking a sandwich. 'She was always a quiet baby you know.'

'Oh mother.'

'Rose here, she has a powerful pair of lungs. Could be an opera singer one day.' Enid looked at her daughter.

'I'm going into business mother.'

'Such ambition.' Enid patted Rose on the knee. 'My girls.'

Over dinner the talk turned to building a house, a museum and Jack Renfrew. Hazel blushed as the chance encounter and subsequent Sunday afternoon was discussed.

'So you think these fellows are the business?' Bill asked helping himself to another spoon of pudding.

'Well, Mr Renfrew said they are world famous. He was quite proud of the fact that he'd secured a position at their practice. He wants to build his owns designs one day.'

'Vuoto and Krickle something?'

'Kartoffelkopf father. It's German. Apparently, Jack said, Mr Kartoffelkopf is practically a genius.'

'Genius eh?'

'Yes Jack said so.'

'This Jack certainly has a lot to say,' Enid gave her husband a dig in the ribs—another silent signal.

'Genius doesn't come cheap,' Bill said. They all sat and contemplated how much genius might cost.

'Still,' Aunt Jane added, 'no harm in having an interview and getting some ideas.'

'Oh, I have plenty of those Jane, plenty!' Bill sat back and brought out his little black book. He patted it, 'plenty.'

CHAPTER 7

Being in the presence of genius might put the average man at a disadvantage. It's not every day you get to sit in the same room with someone of superior intelligence. Bill was about as average as they come, but he had a charm that might mitigate any transgressions.

Mac had ushered the Browns into Mr K office and called for tea. Mr Kartoffelkopf extended his hand and looked over the yokels. He often said he could size up a man in about three minutes. The word in the office was that he was sizing up the clients wallet.

'Come in, sit.'

Bill and Enid looked at the small hideous chairs. They looked like someone had cut the three legs off. The Browns sat and looked up at Mr K behind his desk. Bill squirmed and the chair took umbrage and deposited him on the floor.

'Tarnation.' Bill stood up and dusted off his hat.

'Bill.' Enid blushed and dare not move.

Mr K looked at the Browns and narrowed his eyes. Clearly these Browns were not cultured, nor artistic, or accustomed to mercurial design parameters.

'Ah.' Mr K picked up a pencil.

'Hmm.' Bill countered.

'Mr Kart-offal,' Enid began.

'Kartoffelkopf,' Mr K said.

'Oh, excuse me,' Enid blushed.

'Now listen here Mr Koffelkopf,' Bill put his hands in his pockets and felt his little black book. It gave him courage. 'My wife and I have a plan to move off the farm and build a little house of our own. Something modern, with all the modern conveniences.

'Yes.' Enid said and poked Bill to continue.

'We want something of all those labour saving devices we read about.'

'Yes.' Enid gave her husband another poke.

'Mother wants all the latest.' Bill let the words sink in. And sink in they did. Mr K took his glasses and polished them. He licked his lips and looked at the Browns.

'The farm, ja?'

'Yep, that's right. Sold some land, bought some land, and now we want the easy life. Mother wants what good ol' American knowhow can give. Enid brought out her catalogue and pointed to a washing machine.

'The Orlando Woodrow Automatic Electric washer.'

'Yep. Everybody works but mother,' Bill said,

mimicking the slogan of Mr Woodrow.

Mr Kartoffelkopf had weighed up the Browns and began to get ideas, big ideas.

'Now, I have a few ideas Mr Kart-off.' Bill brought out his little black book, 'just to get you started.'

Architects often cringe at their clients and their few ideas.

Phrases like, 'I just thought we might,' and 'I was wondering if we couldn't just'. Clients who had a simple idea would often have no idea at all if you were to ask an architect's opinion. Mr K naturally came from the position that they were all ignoramuses anyway. He just needed a word for the collective noun. But distain aside, he could be charming when the need arose.

'Mr Brown,' Mr K came around to the front of his desk and sat on the edge in a fatherly sort of pose. He pulled his glasses off and polished them. 'If I am to design a house, ja,' he began, 'no, a home,' he said, 'then I think you need to trust me, ja? 'Your ideas. They are a little bit conventional, don't you think?' Mr K tried to smile. 'We will be married for the duration of the build. You trust Mrs Brown don't you?'

'Naturally.' Bill looked to Enid and smiled. She smiled back.

'Well, I think you need to trust me. I know what I'm doing. I've done it before, ja?'

'Yes but...' Bill began. Mr K held up his hand, 'Ah. Ssshhh.'

'But...'

'Shhh.'

Enid gave her husband a jab and held onto her chair.

'I know what you want, ja. I can sense it.' Mr K rubbed his temples like some sort of clairvoyant. 'I see a home. Electric lights. Washing machine, hot water.'

'Now ya talking.' Bill took the catalogue and flipped to the bath of his dreams.

'It will be a melding of our minds.'

'Really?' Enid shifted ever so slightly on her chair.

'It is possible. Everything is possible Mrs Brown.' Otto Kartoffelkopf's enthusiasm was electrifying.

'Art has no price, ja?'

Mr K picked up his pencil and some paper. He sketched a low roof with a chimney then scrubbed it out. He looked at Mrs Brown perched on the three legged chair and drew a large fireplace, with a brick chimney and a square lounge.

'I see a big family.' Mr K drew a large table.

'Ya got that right.'

Mac came with tea, and Mr Vuoto joined the little party. He raised his eye-brows at the Browns and bowed.

'I am Mr Vuoto.'

'Pleasure.' Bill shook the proffered hand. 'Bill Brown and Mrs Brown.' Mr V smiled.

'Ah, tea, no?' Mr V swooped on the cake.

And the Browns were seduced by modern conveniences at affordable prices. They were bewitched by Mr K's enthusiasm, his go-get-'em drive and his promise to come under budget.

Bill sat back in the Model T with a smile on his face. Hot water, and plenty of it. He could just about smell the soap.

'He seems such a nice man,' Enid said.

There was animated talk at the dinner table that evening in regard to Mr K and Mr V.

'He knew just what we had in mind.'

'He drew a table.'

'He said we should trust him.'

'Like we were married.'

'And he said he knew what we wanted, like a clairvoyant or something.'

'A melding of our minds.'

'Really?' Aunt Jane said.

'That's what the man said.' Bill put a spoonful of pie in his mouth.

Bill Aloysius Brown wouldn't be the first to utter those words, nor would he be the last. Everyone would have their finger in that particular pie.

As with all geniuses, they often forget the small incidentals that crowd the day, although secretaries rarely do. So Mac sent a letter to inform the Browns that if they cared to drop by the office they could pick up a list of buildings and houses that might prove the bona fide of the practice. The letter came by the morning post.

CHAPTER 8

Jack sat back between Mr and Mrs Brown, Aunt Jane was in the driver's seat and Hazel was navigating. It was a regular charabanc.

'Well, isn't this nice,' Enid said as she stuck a very large hat pin into her new hat.

'Yes nice,' Jack smiled and looked at the hat pin. He'd heard young women were defending their honour with pins like that. He didn't have a clue about old women, but with a pin that size he didn't want to take any chances.

'Nice of Mr Kart-offal to give us a guide.' The feather in Enid's hat swung about hitting Jack in the face. He looked at the front seat and sighed.

'Yes, isn't it.' Jack forced a smile at the mangling of Mr K's name and took off his hat.

When Mr K had sent down word that he was to accompany the Browns it was a welcome relief. He'd been rendering the new drawings for the Monash house. Mrs Monash had decided she wanted a reflecting pool in the courtyard. Mr K said, 'naturally' and Jack was drawing cherubs with amphora, and although good at nasturtiums, he wasn't much of an artist with little cherubs.

'And my boy, you might learn something, ja?' Mr K said to Jack as he left with the list of houses for the Browns to admire. Huxley had already primed Jack. Those words by Mr K were coded to mean that a day in the sunshine showing people the talent of V & K was without pay. Every apprentice had been similarly duped at some point in their employment.

The Ford juddered into first gear and Aunt Jane waved her arm about as she merged into the traffic, although merge denotes a smooth transition. It was more like jerk, stop, jerk, stop, neck snap, a bit of whiplash—and they were away.

First stop was the Louis Garrand Museum. They parked across the street and Jack pointed out the salient features trying hard not to be condescending.

'Ya don't say,' Bill tipped back his hat and squinted up at the finials.

'Oh, my.' Enid tipped her head back and her hat enveloped Jack with feathers, flounces and finery.

'They have doors and windows apparently,' Hazel smiled and winked at Jack.

They drove past the Packwell skyscraper, 'Oh my word.'

They practically whizzed past the Noonan Plaza, 'Heavens will you look at that,' And the Postal Tower received a cursory glance, 'Fancy!'

Next on the list was a house which stood on a hill overlooking the city, designed by Mr Kartoffelkopf. It was a low affair that hugged the hill. The building looked so reckless it seemed to threaten pedestrians walking by.

Some people have a condition known as pareidolia. It is the ability to see faces in everyday objects. Now all the occupants of the Model T looked at the house and the house scowled back.

'The Stanwyk residence,' Jack announced as Aunt Jane mounted the curb and they bumped to a halt.

'Will ya look at that,' Bill said. They all looked. The house had portholes that were eyes and an arched doorway which was built like a sneer.

'Rather a lot of bricks aren't there,' Aunt Jane said of the wall that surrounded the house.

'Looks like a prison,' Jane announced and her family readily agreed.

'No son, we don't want a prison.' Bill sat back.

'Or a house that doesn't like us,' Enid added.

The Boorman house was too pointy. The Liebeck residence too flat. The Giedion mansion was...well, too much like a mansion. And then they came to Hula Drive.

'Stop.' Bill pointed as Aunt Jane slammed on the brakes. Jack got a mouthful of feathers; the automobile coming perilously close to a retaining wall that looked like it wouldn't retain a Ford with five occupants in a head on collision.

'That was close,' Jack said.

'Quite,' Hazel blew out the breath she'd been holding.

'Quite exhilarating isn't it.' Aunt Jane adjusted her hat.

And Bill popped a folded bill in Jacks top pocket. 'You're probably not getting paid enough to lose life or limb in an automobile accident.'

Jack mumbled, 'not getting paid at all.'

'Now, that's what I'm talking about.' Bill gestured to a house. They all looked at a lovely little bungalow nestled in a grove of trees.

It looked like a modern home. Not too pointy, a row of square windows in the roofline and a large porch.

'Er, that's not one of V & Ks.' Jack looked over his list. 'We're after number 23.' The occupants of the automobile looked across the street at a house that could only be loosely described as such.

'Oh, hello.' A small gnarled gargoyle of a man waved a rake in the gawkers direction.

'How do.' Bill raised his hat.

'I expect you've come to look at our house.'

'Well...' Bill tried to smile. Even though Enid was on the other side of the seat she still managed to give her husband a poke in the ribs.

'I'll show you around if you like.' The man put down his rake and waited for the troop to file across the suburban road.

'We get people all the time you know,' he said looking at his 'house'. 'A V & K gets attention.'

'Really?' Enid said and received a poke back.

'Oh my word.' Aunt Jane nodded. Hazel and Jack stood back and took it all in. There was a lot to take in.

'Have you lived here long?' Enid asked.

'Not long. I don't like it much myself, but the architect is real proud of it. Calls it urban stone age with Arabic Turkish influence. I sort of just call it ugly.' The styles collided rambunctiously over the façade.

'Oh my giddy aunt.' Enid looked at the house. They took in the round window at knee level, the overhanging upper story that had knobs sticking out of it which looked like oars.

'They're oars,' Mr Preston pointed.

'Oh.' Hazel looked up.

'There,' Jack pointed to an arch. 'That's an arch.' It wasn't much, but it was the only thing that made any architectural sense.

'And that's...well that's a dome thing.' The owner said. They craned their necks to look at the dome thing.

'One of a kind.' Mr Preston stood back and shrugged.

Jack wondered if Mr K was on medication at the time. He couldn't see anything to save the monstrosity except a pair of urns on the parapet.

'Urns,' he said and pointed.

'Sure are,' Mr Preston said. 'Too high to plant anything, but...Mr Kartoffelkopf said I could never have too many urns.' The group looked at the urns and nodded at the words of wisdom.

'I'd invite you in, but...'

'No, that's quite alright,' Aunt Jane said. 'We must get on.'

'Yes. We need to get going.'

'Absolutely, we've got to go.'

The gang made a hasty retreat back to the Ford, bundled in and Nike lived up to her name with

Hazel at the wheel. Enid hung onto her hat as they rounded the corner and it was only when they were finally out of the district did the shock wear off and laughter took its place.

'Can you believe it.'

'Never in my life.'

'Takes all sorts.'

'Ugly.' Enid said.

'The man or the building?' Aunt Jane asked. It was hard to put a cigarette paper between the two.

'And they actually paid money for it.' Bill gave a hoot of laughter.

'Quite a bit actually,' Jack said and this set the group off in howls of laughter once again.

'Tea?'

It sounded like a splendid idea. On Aunt Janes advice Hazel drove to the large park in the centre of the city, and parked the Ford.

'Oh I know just the place.' They followed Aunt Jane to the Fountain Tea Rooms and settled in.

'Did anything we've seen suit you Mr Brown?' Jack asked.

'Well son, I've seen some mighty fine houses, but Mrs Brown and I we have an idea or two of our own.' Bill brought out his little black book and licked his pencil.

He sketched and talked as they watched his small house take on grander proportions. Enid took the pencil and added a room here and there. Bill took up the nub of pencil and wondered if there would be room for a billiard table, as Enid wanted a preserving room.

'I'm sure Mr Vuoto and Mr Kartoffelkopf will be able to accommodate you Mr Brown.' Jack harked back to the Monash solarium and reflecting pool. Anything was possible as long as the client was happy. Jack was yet to discover that happiness might be item 16 on the bill.

'Tell me about the plot Mr Brown.' Jack said.

Bill Brown drew breath and began. He threw his arms about, he gestured to explain the topography, the soil, the solid foundation of stone.

'Father. You got it cheap because it's full of rocks.'

'But they're good rocks.' Bill took a jam tart and popped it in his mouth.

They lobbed back at the office of V & K and Jack followed the Browns up to the office. He held the door for the ladies and Mac looked up and smiled.

'Nice day for it.'

'Lovely,' Enid nodded and her hat bobbled. 'We've had a lovely time, haven't we?' Aunt Jane and Hazel agreed as they looked over the office, the pictures on the walls and the modern furniture.

'Is Mr Kartoffelkopf in?' Jack asked.

'Nope.'

'Mr Vuoto?'

'Nope. They are 'in conference with Mr and Mrs Monash.'

'Right.'

'Something about a fountain.' Mac shook her head. 'Sorry to disappoint you.'

'That's alright Miss. You just tell Mr Kattlehoff that we have seen his houses,' and here Bill winked at his wife and daughter and they giggled, 'and we were mightily impressed.' The women began to stifle giggles with their gloved hands. 'We appreciate Mr Koffletoffs time and list, and we think he'd be just the fellow to give us what we want.'

'Really?'

'Oh, yes.' Bill said. 'We now know what we don't want. Nothing too pointy. Nothing that looks like it doesn't approve of you. Nothing too flat,' and Enid added, 'nothing that looks like it has stone age Arabic things on top.'

'Ah.' Mac understood and nodded. 'You saw the ...'

'We certainly did,' Aunt Jane said and bit her lip to stop a giggle.

'Well, I will pass on your words Mr Brown.'

'Just a house that mother and I can sit back and relax in, knowing it will be fit to busting with modern conveniences.'

'At affordable prices,' Enid ended.

'Right.' Mac wrote it down.

'Well, that's all young lady.' Bill turned to Jack. 'Will we be seeing you again young man?'

'I hope so sir.'

Bill looked at this daughter. 'I do too.'

CHAPTER 9

Jack sat at his drawing table, the Monash house trying to keep his attention. Now Mrs Monash wanted a Porte Cochere that might be more suited to Versailles. His studies came back to him. A Porte Cochere, his professor said, was a fancy name for a doorway that admitted carriages and the like and had a roof. His professor was always putting the fancy into plain language. 'Why complicate the thing,' was his motto. He looked at his drawing. 'Why complicate the thing,' he drew a gabled roof with an urn on top.

He looked up at the clock and the calendar underneath. Another week to pay day. His stomach rumbled at the thin pickings on offer. The time ticked by when, without warning, Mr K breezed into the room. The young men buttoned up their dust coats and looked lively.

'Ah,' Mr K spied Jack in the corner.(*author note, sometimes I just can't help myself*) The word invisible echoed around Jack's head.

'You,' Mr K pointed with his silver topped cane, a new edition to his savoir faire.

'Me,' Jack squeaked.

'I am in need of you, ja.'

'Sir?'

'Come with me, ja.'

Jack stood and hovered. Should he take his coat and hat? Was it just an errand? Did Mr K see something in Jack talent with finials?

'Coat, hat young man.'

'Yes sir.' Jack trotted at the great man's heels as they left the dungeon for sunnier climes.

He came back half an hour later and plopped down at his desk.

'Back so soon,' Huxley stretched and put his pencil down.

'Mr K wanted me to render a small detail in his office. A sun dial.'

'Ah.' Huxley said with a knowing smile.

'What?'

'You've become Mr K's pet. The way Huxley said it, it sounded like a bad thing.

'Is that good?' Jack asked.

'Well...' Swindon began.

'All depends really,' Putney added.

'It's a bit like swallowing a fly,' Steinbeck came into the conversation. 'It happened, you can't change it, and it won't kill you.'

'Right.' Jack said.

'My advice to you Renfrew is to smile, nod and keep your mouth shut.' Huxley took up his pencil.

'Right.' Jack nodded.

'This too shall pass,' Huxley pointed his pencil in the air, 'as the fly assuredly would.'

Over the week Jack was summoned several times to the fourth floor, each time he managed to say as little as possible and nod in all the right places. Every visit was time spent away from his drawings and the all-important placing of his signature on said drawings for something at the end of the month.

'Look,' Huxley pulled Jack over to his desk. He pointed to the small square at the bottom of the blue print. JR was printed next to *drawing by*.

'Roman?'

'My mother is back. Monte Carlo was particularly fruitful. She has bestowed her largess on her dear son.' Huxley smiled and slapped Jack on the back. 'Apparently she missed me.'

'I can't...'

'Yes you can. We all do at times,' Huxley looked at this dungeon companions, 'don't we.'

Steinbeck, Putney and Swindon all nodded.

'Really?'

'Oh yes.' Steinbeck said, 'Jenkins was pet for a while. Played havoc with his work. Still, he built up his thigh muscles running up the stairs. Probably jolly useful on the farm.' Steinbeck slapped his thigh. They all nodded and agreed. Jenkins was a thoroughly nice fellow.

'Well that's really decent of you.'

'Renfrew, you're one of us now.' Huxley gave Jack another slap on the back. 'Anything you need, just ask.'

'Thanks.' Jack sat down and the mail boy, Arlan

popped his head around the door, 'Renfrew.' The lad hoiked his thumb in the direction of the stairs.

'Go forth young man, conquer and vanquish,' Huxley theatrically waved his pencil in the air.

Mr K stood behind his desk and held up a letter.

'These people, they are your people.'

'Pardon.'

Mr K squinted at the letter. 'Brown, ja?'

'Mr and Mrs Brown sir?'

'That's what I said. Brown. An unfortunate name, but there you have it.'

'My people sir?'

'Ja. Your people.'

'No sir.'

'You are from farming I think.'

'Well, yes.'

'Your people.' Mr K said with conviction. 'The salt of the earth, ja?'

'Yes sir.'

'They are bothering me.'

'Yes sir.'

'They say...' and Mr K read the salient points of the letter that Bill had dictated to Rose and Rose had typed up at her college.

Bill was accustomed to things moving at a fair clip. He was familiar with the maxim of 'get the job done'. The letter noted that they had met Mr K and were given an undertaking that he could design a house. So where, Bill wrote was the contract, the design, the beginnings of his dream home?

'Where indeed,' Mr K said. 'Tell your people that the word of Otto Kartoffelkopf is contract enough. Tell your people that a man of genius doesn't need distractions.'

'Yes sir.'

'And Mr Renfrew,'

'Yes sir?'

'I want you to go.'

'Yes sir.' Jack made to leave.

'No. I want you to go to this little bit of land, ja? I want you to tell me what you see. If the Browns want genius, I need to know where to put it.'

'Yes sir.' Jack ground his teeth. More time wasted. 'Er,'

'Ja?' Mr K looked like he might be receptive. He was in an expansive, happy mood.

'I was wondering Mr Kartoffelkopf, is this surveying trip an opportunity to learn something, or perhaps ...' Jack swallowed—hard. 'Perhaps as part of my duties it will be attracting recompense.'

'Recompense?' Mr K said it like a dirty word.

'Yes sir. Recompense.'

'Ah. A young man. A lady perhaps? Something to impress.'

'Yes sir.'

'Ah to be young.' Mr K closed his eyes and smiled. 'You shall have your recompense Mr Renfrew.

'Thank you sir.'

Mac listened as Jack outlined his duties. She nodded and took notes.

'Did Mr K say how you were to get there?'

'No.'

'Did Mr K say where you will stay?'

'No.'

'Did Mr K say who was going to pay.'

'No.'

'Ah.' Mac tapped her pencil on her ink blotter.

'You don't mean...'

'I think I do.' Mac shook her head. 'Renfrew I think you might just break even.'

Jack's shoulders slumped.

'Mr V is busy with the Monash house. He's notoriously tight with the purse strings.' Mac looked at Jack and a rush of motherly love came over her. 'Look, leave it with me. I'll see what I can do.'

'Thanks.'

Back at the dungeon Jack outlined his dilemma. The others listened and commiserated.

'Tough luck eh,' Swindon said.

'Rotten I'd say,' Putney added.

Steinbeck put a dollar on Jacks table. 'It's all I have, sorry.'

'Thanks fellas.

Huxley clicked his fingers. 'Mr Renfrew if this isn't your lucky day.'

'Roman?'

'I have an automobile. Just sitting there. You can drive I suppose.'

'Yes.'

'And you know the value of a loan I suppose.'

'I do.'

'All for one and one for all d'Artagnan.' Huxley waved his pencil like a sword. 'But first we need to discuss the finer details.'

'If you say so,' Jack said while thinking having friends was just about the finest thing a fellow could have. He'd yet to fall in love, and that would put a whole different perspective on things.

The finer details required a pot of tea and as chance would have it, the company of Hazel Brown. Roman, Hazel and Jack sat in the Fountain Tea Rooms and went over the plans.

'If you could come to my mother's apartment around six, I can give you the keys to the jalopy. Mother wants to meet you.' Huxley patted Jack's hand. 'I may have said some things about you Jack. She may have the impression that you are just the sort of guiding influence her wayward son needs.

'Me?'

'That's about the size of it.'

'You could tell her all about doors and windows Jack.' Hazel raised her eyebrow and sipped her tea.

'And you'd be doing me a grand favour Jack if you'd just mention that you're from Italian extraction.'

'Me?'

'Yes, Sort of Lucria's brother perhaps.' Huxley turned to Hazel. Lucria is the love of my life. Mother likes introductions and such. A bit old fashioned like that.' Huxley judged on merit not reputation, although if the ladies had any say they'd always go for the latter rather than the former.

'Oh, I see.' Hazel looked at Jack. 'He doesn't look terribly Italian.'

'It can't be helped.' Roman helped himself to a scone. 'Mother is quite the bohemian, although she is prone to flights of fancy. I remember a Greek fellow. Spouted poetry and philosophy and such. Father had a devil of a time getting rid of him.'

He looked at Hazel and then turned to Jack, then back to Hazel. 'Miss Brown. Be on your guard. Artistic types will seduce you with their long hair and fancy language. The city is full of them.'

'I think I'd rather be seduced by intelligence Mr Huxley.'

'Or money?' Huxley said,' it comes in handy now and again.'

'I should think Miss Brown quite capable of judging someone's character in a snap.' Jack said. Hazel wasn't quite sure if it was a compliment or an insult.

'Never-the-less.' Huxley wagged his finger. 'Now, where were we?'

'At your mother's.'

'Ah.' Well just pave the way Renfrew. I will do the rest.'

'I'll try.' Jack said.

'And in return you will have the automobile. To unpathed waters, undreamed shores.' Huxley put his hand on his heart, 'that's the Bard.'

Jack looked at Hazel, 'And then I will come and get you,'. First thing in the morning.' Hazel nodded.

'You know you could stay at the farm. There's plenty of room and you'd save money.'

'I wouldn't want to impose.' Jack hoped he *could* impose. As it was, he had borrowed money from Huxley, Steinbeck and Swindon, who'd found a dollar and fifty cents.

'Mother and father don't want to waste their return ticket. Father is rather a stickler for getting his monies worth.'

Oh how those words would reverberate as Bill dreamed of hot water and bath plugs.

Hazel poured a second cup of tea for the young men. 'They will take the train, but I think we'll get home first. Three hours as the crow flies.'

'Just point the way,' Jack said and as he thought on the jaunt ahead he had a feeling it would be fun, enjoyable and amusing. Three hours in the company of Miss Hazel Brown in an automobile might just be enough to cement their friendship into something more.

'And I would suppose you'll stay on the farm?' Jack asked Hazel.

'Yes I suppose.' They looked at the tea pot.

'The country air and all that.' Huxley said.

'Yes.' Hazel sighed. 'Of course...'

'Yes?' Jack sat up.

'If I had a job.'

'A job?' Jack pursed his lips. 'Can you type?'

'No.'

'Book keeping?'

'No.'

'Sew?'

'No.' Hazel fiddled with her tea cup.

Jack couldn't think of anything else.

'What about music?' Huxley asked.

'No.' Hazel shook her head.

'Aunt Jane's almost a competent driver now. So she doesn't need me.'

'Wait,' Jack took Hazel's hand. 'Why don't you start a school? For driving. For ladies. You said Aunt Jane appreciated the lessons.'

'Yes.'

'She said you were a natural.'

'Yes.'

'Well?' Jack looked at his hand holding hers, 'Excuse me,' he pulled away.

'I suppose I could.'

'Of course you could. I'm sure plenty of young—and old women want lessons.' Huxley said.

'They probably do.'

'I know a few game girls—with automobiles.' Huxley brought out his small wallet for calling cards. 'I could introduce you.'

'Really?'

'Leave it to me.' Huxley patted Hazel's hand.

It didn't take long before it all came together. And the bonus for Jack was Miss Hazel Brown was staying in the city, which made the city a much more agreeable place.

And Brown's Driving School for Adventurous Ladies was born. The acronym for the graduation certificate an unfortunate co-incidence. Brown's Adventurous Driver!

Mrs Huxley greeted Jack with enthusiasm.

'Roman has told me so much about you Mr Renalto.'

'Si.' Jack smiled and tried not to sweat.

'An architect.'

'Si.'

'And so young.

'Si.'

'Dear Roman.' Mrs Huxley looked at her son, 'we had high hopes. No talent apparently.'

'No.' Jack shrugged.

'And your sister Mr Renalto?'

'Si. Lucria.'

'Yes. You must bring her to tea one afternoon. If you can spare the time.'

Jack bowed and waved his hand in the air as he'd seen Mr Vuoto do.

'Do you know the Stotto's from Turin?'

'No. Sorry.'

'The Gravini's from Florence?'

'Sorry.'

Mrs Huxley frowned and looked at the son.

'Are you sure?'

'Oh mother. Not everyone runs in your circles. Mr Renalto designs houses and such. He probably doesn't have time to flit about.'

'No.' Jack just wanted the time to leave. 'I really should be going, he said.

Huxley handed over the keys to his Pierce-Arrow 66.

'I owe you Jack.'

'Roman, I think I owe you.' Jack looked over the automobile.

'Now, there is extra gas in the trunk and I think you'll find the experience quite thrilling. Sixty-six horses so they say.'

'Sixty-six.' Jack whistled. 'I'll be back the day after tomorrow. I'll come straight to work?'

'If you could drop it at mother's that might work. She's got a garage.'

'Right.'

'Have fun,' Huxley stood back as Jack put the beast into gear and slowly drove away.

Taking care of someone else's automobile can be a nerve wracking experience. Jack spent the whole night sleeping with his elbows on his window ledge looking at the vehicle parked outside his bedsit. Not that he lived in a neighbourhood that was prone to theft, but one can never be too careful.

As morning dawned, he woke up with a start and rubbed the back of his neck. It only took a minute to come to his senses and look outside. The Pierce-Arrow was still there. A pigeon was sitting on the roof.

'Get,' Jack shouted. It was going to be a hellish drive to the country. Country roads were full of stones, bushes and wildlife.

With his pencils, sketch pad, a theodolite in a suitcase Jack packed his overnight bag and put the lot in the automobile. It was then he discovered the small valise in the trunk. Roman had provided a set of clothes for the country with a small note of thanks. What Roman thought was the country and where Jack was going were two different things. White flannels, a boater and a smart white blazer might do for a country house owned by the Vanderbilt's, but a block of land?—that required rubber boots.

Someone said, you don't really know a person until you've been in traffic with them. One should add in traffic with a borrowed automobile that costs more than your yearly wage. Hazel gritted her teeth as Jack inched his way along the road, hunched over the wheel.

Another road user honked their Klaxon and made a rather rude suggestion where Jack might put the tyre jack.

'I think they want you to go a little faster.'

'I think I know how to drive Miss Brown.' Under considerable stress, a man (or woman) are liable to say just about anything.

Hazel adjusted her hat and gave a huff.

'What!' Jack snapped.

'Nothing.' Hazel crossed her arms and stoically looked ahead. As we discussed earlier when one has a knowledge of something and is eager to impart that knowledge the temptation to be condescending is endless.

The automobile crawled along and was passed by a dog trotting on the sidewalk.

'When I said three hours Mr Renfrew, I thought we'd be travelling a little faster.'

'That's alright for you to say. This isn't my automobile.'

'I realise that,' Hazel said. 'Never-the-less I think you should drive a little more assertively. Other road users are accustomed to driving at a safe speed.'

'Assertively.' Jack hugged the side of the road and slowed down for a small rock. It was a pebble in reality, but these things can often get out of proportion when you are being nagged by your passenger.

'Yes. Assertively. I think you will find your gear changes improve and your confidence too.'

'I'm not one of your adventurous ladies Miss Brown.

'Not adventurous at all.' Hazel quipped.

'I suppose you can do better?'

'As a matter of fact...'

'Tosh.'

'Bumkin.'

'Tarnation.'

'Codswallop.'

They traded insults as the limits of the city came into view.

'You will need to turn right at the junction. It's signposted to Boydsville.'

'Boydsville.' Jack repeated as he gripped the steering wheel like a man hanging onto his last pay cheque.

The junction was negotiated, they were out into the country and Jack relaxed, just a little.

He took a large dose of fresh air through his nostrils. 'Excuse me Miss Brown. I apologise.'

'Quite alright. Although your swearing has a long way to go to beat my Aunt Jane.'

'Really?'

'Like a sailor.'

'My word.' Jack exclaimed.

'Or about a dozen of hers.' Hazel laughed.

The countryside is quite relaxing. Fresh air, sunshine, cows, fields and the endeavours of man as far as the eye can wander.

The pair sat in silence, except for the noise of the engine, just enjoying the view. For two people who were practically weaned on fresh air, it was like coming home. Jack had tried hard to escape, but now he felt a kinship with the cows, the fences, the smell of manure. Hazel felt she could enjoy it while knowing she didn't need to stay and work at it. She had a job, a business, a new life.

Jack stretched his back in the seat and flexed his shoulders.

'Would you like me to take the wheel?' Hazel had been waiting for the moment when Jack might tire. She was itching to get behind the wheel.

It sounded like a perfectly good suggestion. They had two hours ahead and leaf springs, leather upholstery and wood panels can only soften the ride so much.

'Well...'

'I'm quite capable Mr Renfrew—Jack.'

'Oh I don't doubt that. It's just that...'

'What? That I'm a woman. Is that it?'

Jack stole a look at Hazel. He knew he shouldn't say it. He told himself he should just keep his mouth closed. He willed his tongue to keep still. It didn't help.

'It's perfectly reasonable to assume that women are not as adept at the intricacies of the automobile... yet. The combustion engine is a complicated piece of machinery.'

'I don't know how to make a teapot, but I can use one.'

'You see. A teapot is nothing like the internal combustion engine.'

'For instance, do you know...' Jack began when he saw Hazel was sulking and looking out of the window. 'Huxley would probably never forgive me if we had an accident.'

Hazel turned, 'But we're not going to have an accident.'

'You say that now, but...'

'Jack.'

'Yes.'

'Let me drive...please.' The last word came out a bit more of a bleat than Hazel would have liked, but she added a smile and a gloved hand on Jack's arm. Women might have an arsenal of tactics up their sleeve, but invariably they fall back on tried and trusted methods of persuasion.

'Please Jack.' Hazel pursed her lips and put her dimple to good use.

'Alright.' He pulled over and left the engine running. They changed places. Hazel familiarised herself with the levers, pedals and dials.

'It's a bit tricky at first,' Jack said, but he didn't get any further as Hazel put her foot down and used every horse available. All Jack could do was hang on.

Her gear changes were impeccable, her steering first class and her command of the automobile, faultless. Hazel smiled and began to enjoy herself.

It didn't take Jack long before he relaxed and began to talk—probably more than he ordinarily would, but that is the nature of, well nature; the birds and the bees and being in the country with the birds and the bees.

'A farm,' Hazel said.

'A scholarship,' Hazel nodded.

'Top marks,' she exclaimed.

'V & K, on your first interview,' she raised her eyebrows and whistled.

'His pet,' she frowned.

'So I've got to prove myself. With your parent's house. It's my chance you see.'

'Oh father is quite easy to get along with Jack.' Hazel negotiated a pot hole in the road. 'He's a simple man with simple needs. Mother is the stickler. Fight to the death for her family and all that sort of thing.'

'Right.'

'Just a nice house, with all those labour saving devices.' Hazel turned onto a dirt road and pulled up at a row of small houses and a shop.

'Shall we eat?'

Jack thought of the money in his pocket. It would need to last, especially if he couldn't stay at the Brown's for free.

'Just a sandwich.'

The remainder of the journey was with convivial company.

'All your life on the farm,' Jack said.

'A big family.' Jack nodded.

'Ten,' he exclaimed.

'A house of their own,' Jack raised his eyebrows.

'Something different rather than a farmhouse.' He frowned. He'd seen something different on Hula Street.

'Well I'm sure Mr V or Mr K will come up with something.

'Not too sure on urban stone age though.' Hazel said.

'No, definitely not urban stone age.'

They laughed and it wasn't long before they pulled into chez Brown, four barking dogs, a water-pump and well in the front yard, a broken tractor on a jack and a pig on the porch.

'Home.'

Jack could see the need for modern conveniences at affordable prices.

It was at the kitchen table that evening Jack found the true worth of people like the Browns. They were, what the papers described as home grown. He ate a hearty meal, had two helpings of pudding and settled back with the Browns a contented fellow. The kerosene lamps were lit, the stove was popping and crackling nicely and the kettle a quiet whistle on the side. Yes, the country was quite comfortable, restful and relaxing when you didn't have endless chores to do.

'So you're from farming,' Bill said as he took the tea pot and filled his cup.

'That's right.' Jack helped himself to a slice of cake.

'What sort?' Bill asked.

You may not know, but even in farming there is a hierarchy, and every farmer thinks his chosen field on top. Wheat farmers deride sorghum. Dairy scoff at pig. Pig roll their eyes at chicken and turkey comes somewhere near the bottom with vegetables. Where the natural order actually sits is anyone's guess.

So for Bill to casually ask, 'what sort?' was the sort of loaded question that might have a young man cough as if instead of sponge cake he'd swallowed a boiled egg.

'My Uncle Fred was...' Jack looked at Hazel. She mouthed beans and shook her head. There was a whole story about Mr Brown and beans, one far too long to discuss now.

'He was beets.'

'Beets eh.' Bill digested the word. He and pigs might be the only ones that can.

'That's it. Beets.'

'Never had much call for beets myself.' Bill took a sip of his tea.

'You can use the tops and the bottom,' Jack said.

'Fancy,' Enid began to clear the table.

Uncle Fred and Jack, and 'beets'.

'You'll be in the boys room Mr Renfrew,' Enid handed Jack a goose down quilt and a pillow. Fourth door on the left.

'Good night Mr Renfrew.' Hazel passed Jack on the landing.

'Oh, goodnight Miss Brown.' Jack smiled and looked at Enid.

'This is very kind of you Mrs Brown. I really didn't expect...'

'Nonsense my boy.' Enid patted the quilt, 'never mind father, he doesn't know his onions from his beets. Now you have a good night's sleep and in the morning after a decent breakfast we'll go and see that bit of land we have in mind.'

Jack went to his bed, fourth door on the left and dreamed of bacon and eggs, griddle scones, jam and honey, coffee and hot rolls. Yes my word, the country was charming, quite charming when there wasn't a beet in sight.

CHAPTER 10

Oh give me a home where the buffalo roam, so the song goes in the Cowboy ballad, but Bill Brown's piece of paradise didn't have buffalo in mind. The Parson quarter acre was an undulating, rocky piece of land that a cowboy wouldn't waste spit on.

'I figure son, we'd build here,' Bill spread his arms wide to take in the outcrop of rock that looked older than Moses, the creek which might be prone to flooding, the stretch of bog and the numerous igneous rocky outcrops like a sixteen year old's pimples.

'Er, here?'

'That's the idea,' Bill kicked a stone. 'Solid foundations.'

'Yes.'

Jack wondered how much it would cost to dig those solid foundations. 'Mr Brown.'

'Hmmm.' Bill was already pacing out his

bathroom.

'I wonder if you have really thought this through?'

'Yep.'

'I mean, this is a lovely view and everything, but the land, the time, the money.'

That last word got ol' Bill's attention. 'Money?'

'Well, it will take some digging; these rocks look igneous to me.'

Bill looked at his rocks. He imagined his house standing on its igneous foundations for years to come.

'What-ever it takes son.' Some words often come back to haunt one, no matter how hard you try to wriggle out of admitting you said them.

Jack had yet to realise architectural practice invariably means spending someone else's money.

Jack took measurements. He employed his theodolite with Bill holding the level. He sketched the area and put arrows on the possible obstructions. And all the while Bill looked on.

'Know what you're doing son?'

'Yes thanks.'

'I have a few ideas myself.'

'Really?' It was a word that sounded like an invitation to Bill.

'Here, just let me have that pencil will you?'

In hindsight Jack regretted handing over his pencil. At the time it was just good manners. After all, he was eating the man's food, sleeping under the man's roof and...trying to woo the man's daughter.

Bill went to town drawing his house. It had acres of rooms, more windows than Hardwick Hall and of course a bathroom that a Roman Emperor would be proud to use.

'Of course it's not to scale son, but you get the idea.'

Oh yes, Jack got the idea.

Mr Brown's little piece of paradise was beginning to resemble the Monash residence.

The drive back to the city was a good time to consolidate one's thoughts. Jack's thoughts were of Miss Brown, and no matter how hard he tried to think of architecture, houses, finials and porte cocheres, his mind turned to Hazel.

She'd come back to the city once her effects were packed. Her school would be a success. They would celebrate their good fortune, he'd build a house for the Browns and life would be rosy. It all looked so simple.

Good ideas rarely are.

With the automobile dropped off at Mrs Huxley's Jack took the trolley to work and went to the dungeon. He'd managed to save all the money and handed it back with thanks all round.

'Good trip?'

'Marvellous.' Jack smiled. 'Simply marvellous,' he handed out the home made cakes Mrs Brown had foisted upon him.

'The Arrow?' Huxley asked.

'Drives like a dream.'

'No, I mean no accidents or anything?'

'Not a one.' Jack said and patted Huxley on the back.

'Mr K's been asking for you. I think he forgot he sent you to the country.' Swindon said.

'Oh.'

'Yes, came down here several times.' Putney added.

'You should go upstairs Renfrew.' Steinbeck licked his fingers.

'Right.'

Mac looked over Jack and raised her eyebrow. 'Someone's happy. Have a good time?'

'Yes. Quite good thanks. Is Mr K in?'

'Go right in, he's just having his afternoon tea.'

When you are in a good mood, the world is a lovely place and everything is just fine and dandy it's hard to understand that not everyone is full of sweetness and light. Jack breezed into a threatening storm.

'Mr Kartoffelkopf,' Jack began to rifle through his notes, 'I have the relevant facts regarding the Brown site.'

'Where have you been.'

'To the country.'

'The country? I pay you to be here,' Mr K railed. Jack thought the last statement a hit below the belt. He actually paid for his own trip, his own pencils and to be frank he hadn't been paid...yet.

'But you told me to go to the country. To see the Brown site.'

'I did?'

'Yes sir.'

There was a moment of quiet as the two looked at one another.

'Well?' Mr K sipped his tea.

Jack launched into his evaluation of the elevation, the substrate, the igneous rocks and the stream. He showed his wonderful drawings, his measurements and his calculations. It was a fine job. A job to be proud of. Mr K thought it a little too thorough, a little too precise, and just a little too much like talent. One genius was enough for the practice.

'So, what do you think?' Here was another one of those loaded questions. Apprentices aren't paid to think, Steinbeck, Swindon, Putney and Huxley had drilled that maxim into Jack.

'Well...' he began. 'The client, Mr Brown said, whatever it takes.'

Mr K smiled. As we mentioned, architects are adept at spending other people's money.

Mr K often has flashes of brilliance. That's what he would call it if ever he wrote his autobiography. His brilliance might be described as recycling to those that are not accustomed to genius.

Otto had seen something in The Architectural Review in the late 1890s. His mind had thought on it—he'd drawn something in the 1900s and no-one would dare build it—for a good ten years or so.

So, there it sat, until a sucker—oops sorry—a man of ideas, a forward thinker, a man who had a quarter acre consisting largely of rocks might cross the threshold.

Bill Brown was that man.

Otto could see an opportunity when it was presented. Even genius has a practical view when necessary. Mr K often handed out drawings of his ideas like 5c cigars, because as every architectural genius knows, everyone else is unable to draw above kindergarten level.

Now the eureka moment of genius only managed Mr V and Mac as an audience, they'd seen it all before.

The Monashs were given the opportunity to partake of genius. They declined.

The Boormans said no.

The Leibecks ran and didn't reappear for a month.

The Gideons? Well Mr Gideon went and died. No-one could be sure he didn't do it out of spite after he said yes, just so he wouldn't live to regret it.

And so, Torheit was dusted off once again, for Mr K liked to name his creations as if they were his babies.

That the German word translated to folly was just a co-incidence. A better name might have been Verrücktheit, craziness.

Mr Vuoto patted his partner on the back. 'If you get it built, I eat my hat, no'

And what did it look like I hear you ask? Well, if you can imagine an apple crate turned upside down and standing on legs you can't go wrong. The gaps between the slats are windows and that's about it. One wonders what exactly Otto did see in The

Architectural Review in 1890 and if it wasn't an advertisement for Jim Dandy Apples.

'The conquest of the flat surface, ja,' Mr K said standing on his metaphorical soap box, which was not unlike an apple box. He spread his drawing on the table.

'Genius, ja?' Mr K said

'Genius, no?' Mr V said.

In due course Torheit was sent down to the dungeon to be resurrected. There was a groan from the apprentices as they saw the apple crate once again.

'Really?' Steinbeck said.

'Not again,' Putney moaned.

All Swindon could do was grunt. They had over the life of the drawings added blinds, taken away blinds, put in a chimney, taken it out again and given it a more appealing look with a trailing vine.

Jack read over the notes attached to the scrolls of plans.

TORHEIT

A house that takes advantage of the many efficient industrial products and omits dust gathering doodads.

Jack was to render the façade to make it look modern, new, exciting.

'Add an urn,' Huxley suggested.

A whistle from the door made the apprentices look up. The mail boy swung off the door knob and called for Jack.

'He wants ya.'

Once again Jack took to the stairs.

Mr K and Mr V had the plans for Torheit on their drawing board.

'Ah. The farmer.' Mr K indicated Jack should hold his coloured pencils and his T square. It wasn't exactly the promotion Jack had in mind.

'Watch.' Mr K said and took off his glasses to polish them. Mr V started to make a list of consumables as the 'genius' replaced his glasses and fiddled with his triangle then drew a few lines.

'We will build into the hill.'

'Yes sir, but it might be a bit difficult. There are quite a few rocks. I took the opportunity to look at the geological survey. It's a large shelf.' Jack studied the plans.

'This,' Jack pointed to a pylon, 'might need deep footings.

Mr V wrote it down.

'It will be autochthonous.'

'Pardon sir?'

'Autochthonous.' If there is one thing to decimate the talented opposition it is big words, or so Mr Kartoffelkopf thought. For those of us whose diet doesn't include swallowing dictionaries, autochthonous means 'of the area and formed in its present position'.

'You will project manage this, ja' Mr K threw his hand over the plans. 'You know these people. They are your people.' Mr K was adept at delegation, especially when it could quite easily be called passing the buck or the hot kartoffel.

'Salt of the earth, no?'

'Salt of the earth,' Jack said.

The sword of Damocles had fallen, and now Mr K was rubbing salt into the wound.

'Project manager,' Huxley said. 'Lucky you.'

'Why did he pick me?'

Huxley looked at Putney who looked at Steinbeck who glanced at Swindon

'Er,' Swindon said.

'I think Swindon is trying to elucidate something of a poisoned chalice,' Huxley offered.

'Busy,' Steinbeck said and bent over his drawing board.

'Not my forte really,' Putney said, adding, 'coloured pencils more my line.'

'And don't forget Mr Renfrew, you're country stock—salt of the earth and all that,' Huxley smiled.

'And Mr K's pet,' Swindon added.

Jack looked up. He was sure the sword of that Damocles fellow was hovering right above his head. Project manager didn't sound like a step up the corporate ladder, more like sticking his neck out for the chop.

'You might have declined,' Putney offered.

'Well, you see...' Jack began, 'I'm so in love with digestion and the 'art' of living I said yes.'

Swindon sniggered. 'I think Edgar's living in California now.'

'Edgar?'

'Last project manager.' Putney said.

'On the Gideon mansion.' Huxley interjected.

'Poor fellow went bald,' Steinbeck added.

Jack ran his fingers through his hair.

CHAPTER 11

'Modern.' Jack stood back and let the Browns take in the drawing of Torheit.

'Torheit? What does that mean?'

'I really can't say Mr Brown. Mr Kartoffelkopf likes to name his houses.'

'Modern you say?' Bill scratched his head.

'Oh yes, very.'

'Bit brutal, isn't it?'

The building was brutal to look at. If it wasn't an architectural term it should have been. Bill would need to wait until the 1950s to apply the word Brutalism.

'With all the conveniences you say.'

'Absolutely.'

'What do you think Enid?' Bill took out his spectacles and had a good long look at the drawing. Jack had done his best. It really was a splendid drawing as far as apple crates can look splendid.

'I don't know about such things, but I just

wonder where the front door might be?'

'The front door?' Jack winced as if he'd walked into a door.

'Yes.' Enid frowned and looked a little closer.

'It's sort of...well...around there,' Jack pointed at a clever deception of the eye. The front door masked into invisibility.

'Oh.' Enid sat down.

'And the bathroom?'

'Here,' Jack pointed to a room on the plan that looked like a linen closet.

Bill shook his head. 'That'll never do.'

'It won't?' Jack asked.

The little black book was produced and Bill schooled Jack on the dimensions of a bath from Mr McCreedy's Porcelain Emporium. 'Need elbow room.'

'Right.'

Enid stood and put her two cents worth in, 'a linen closet needs to have room for my quilts, and an airing rack would be nice.' She fetched her catalogue and flipped to the relevant page. 'It's hygienic you know.'

'Is it?' Jack nodded.

Enid took a good look at the plans. She traced the rooms with her finger and squinted at the tiny figures denoting the size.

'These bedroom look a bit big.'

'Big?' Jack said and swallowed.

'Yes, big. Don't you think they are big father?'

Bill looked at the plans. He squinted, turned to Jack, 'big.'

Enid Brown was a sensible sort of woman.

All she wanted was a normal size bedroom with a normal size bed. Mr K had the idea the master bedroom would be a statement room, a very large one.

'Big.' It was Bill's last word on the matter...for now.

The washing machine, drapes, electrical outlets and swing hammock were discussed. The kitchen sink, hot water and stove were debated and the need for screens on the windows thought a necessity.

Jack finished the list, 'is that about it?'

'Just one more thing,' Bill took up a pencil and pointed.

'How about a porch?'

'A porch?'

'A man needs a porch.'

'I'll let Mr Kartoffelkopf know.'

'You do that son. I think we can get this sorted, as long as it is modern.' Bill put away his little black book. 'And just let me know how much it might be. Down to the dollar.'

'Down to the dollar.'

'That's right. Then Mrs Brown and I know where we stand.'

By the time Mr Vuoto had finished with the estimates, Bill might need to sit down.

Fronting Mr K with the Brown's suggestions was akin to going into the lion's den with a lamb chop strapped to your chest.

'A porch.'

'Philistines.'

'A bigger bathroom.'

'Impossible.'

'A linen closet with an airing rack.'

'Madness.'

'Electrical outlets for a washing machine.'

'Maybe.'

'Mrs Brown suggested inside the house, next to the kitchen. Sort of handy, she said.'

'Handy,' Mr K threw up his hands. 'Insanity.'

Jack ran his fingers through his hair. He was beginning to understand why Edgar was in California, without hair.

'A telephone.'

'Ich glaub mich knutscht ein elch!'

'Pardon sir?'

The look Mr K gave Jack just about translated the German. It actually means 'I believe I've been kissed by an elk—and who wouldn't be surprised, but in normal parlance it translates to 'I can't believe it.'

Mr K had no concept of American family life. People actually want to be comfortable in their home. They want to relax, take their shoes off, put their feet up and think themselves jolly lucky to be alive. They don't want sharp angles that catch ones hip every time they round the corner to the bathroom. They don't want acres of floor space to cross to get their slippers or a box of matches, and they don't particularly want three legged chairs.

'And Mr Brown said he'd like an estimate, down to the dollar.' Mr K's eyebrows shot up, he pulled his glasses off and rubbed furiously. Another one of those expressions that really don't need any explanation, although Mr K took a deep breath and Jack had to listen to about five minutes of aggrandizement, the gist of, didn't the Brown's appreciate they were getting the work of genius. Heck, they should be paying him.

Mr V had a bit more to say on the matter. Although bi-lingual, the string of Italian words coming from his office and the volume left no doubt what he thought about Bill's 'down to the dollar.' Jack left the office with his ears ringing and a new vocabulary.

In due course Mr Vuoto with his finger held high in the air and saying 'the union of geometry and imagination,' came up with a figure. His estimates were at the mercy of his imagination.

Jack was given the unenviable task of breaking the news to Mr Brown.

'Good luck,' Huxley said as Jack gathered the drawings, the estimates and the renderings—still without a porch.

'Do you have next of kin?' Steinbeck asked.

'Remember, you can always go to California.' Putney added.

'And you still have a head of hair.' Swindon finished.

Jack walked out of the building with more than a modicum of dread. He was going to catch the trolley when one of those fortuitous co-incidences happened and Hazel drove by and waved. Jack wasn't to know she'd been circling the block

waiting for him. She'd telephoned the office of V &
K and knew he would be on his way.

'Oh hello,' Hazel leaned out of the Ford.

'Miss Brown.' Jack juggled the plans.

'Need a ride Mr Renfrew?'

If Hazel had been offering a lobotomy, Jack
would jump at the chance.

'What timing. Thank you Miss Brown. I presume
you are on your way to Mrs Parkers residence?'

'Oh yes.' Hazel patted the passenger seat, 'get
in—(said the spider to the fly).'

'How's the business?' Jack asked.

'Fine.'

'You?' Hazel asked.

'Fine.'

'Settled in?'

'Yes, thanks.' Hazel made a left turn.

'I've got your parent's plans.'

'Yes, I see that.'

'Your parents are at Mrs Parker's house?'

'I know.'

'Of course you do.' Jack fiddled with his hat.

There is a fine line in the game of courtship. One
doesn't want to appear eager, but on the other hand
one doesn't want to appear aloof. Hazel wasn't
quite sure which was winning. She'd been eager
once before and look how that ended—at the altar.

Jack felt, at this stage, it would be easier to woo
the parents.

The Browns looked at the drawings. Aunt
Jane looked at the drawings. Hazel looked at the
drawings.

'It's very modern,' Aunt Jane said.

'Yes modern,' Hazel smiled at Jack.

'Mr Kartoffelkopf can assure you it is unique.'

'I don't doubt that son.'

'It's a lovely drawing father.' Hazel had spied the initials in the corner.

'Oh, yes,' Enid said, 'a lovely drawing.'

'So well drawn,' Aunt Jane pointed to an urn.

'And here,' Jack unfurled the plans, 'you will have room to add all the modern conveniences you want.'

Bill looked at the acres of space and not a dividing wall to be seen.

'Roomy.'

'I see that son.'

'Oh, and here is the bathroom. Mr Kartoffelkopf has extended it, for your bath.'

'Now ya getting the idea.' Bill peered at the bathroom. It was labelled, *Gentleman's bathroom.*

'Mr Kartoffelkopf said a porch would spoil the spatial plane and the symbolic strength of the inherent beauty of simplicity.' It was a mouthful, but Bill swallowed it. He nodded at the simplicity. He traced his finger over the symbolic strength and looked for the inherent beauty.

'People will talk of *Torheit* for years to come.' Jack said. 'An icon.'

'An icon eh?'

'Yes sir.'

'Father, you will have an icon. Mr Parson doesn't have an icon.' There was quite a bit of tit for tat in Brownsville when it came to the Browns and the Parsons.

'Well...' Bill began. The assembled crowd held

their breath.

'If it's an icon, with modern conveniences, well,' Bill scratched his head, 'I suppose,' he puffed out his chest, 'whatever it takes.' He looked at the estimate and wondered what the going rate for an icon was these days, because he was paying top dollar for his.

CHAPTER 12

The engineer cast his eye over Torheit and filed a report.

It could be built—anything is possible.

It might be sound—miracles happen.

And,

It would need something more than wishful thinking come the first winter storm. A flat roof and snow don't always get along.

Mr K looked at the report. He had a few words to say about engineers. They weren't nice ones.

Jack was summoned once again.

'The weather.'

'Pardon sir?'

'The weather. What about the weather.'

'I think it might rain this afternoon sir.' Jack stooped to look out the window.

Mr K was perilously close to calling Jack an idiot. He pulled the engineers report from his papers and pointed.

Jack read the report, or enough of it to put two and two together.

'Ah. The weather.'

'Ja. Torheit is my creation. It must be born.'

'Yes sir.'

'Well? The weather?'

'I think it's just sort of, well, really when it all boils down, and not to put too finer point on it, it really is just about...'

'Ja?' Mr K waited.

'Typical for the topography.' Jack tried to look informed, intelligent and ingratiating.

'We will put the sloping roof, ja?'

'Ja,' Jack said.

And so the plans were amended once again. And once again a groan of anguish was heard in the dungeon.

'You know,' Jack began, 'I had an idea that if we put a false roof over the existing roof it might act like a patio. The Browns could sit up there and admire the view.'

'Are you completely mad,' Huxley asked.

'Too much sun perhaps?' Swindon said.

'This is Torheit. Mr K's pet project.' Putney added.

'You don't mess with genius Renfrew, unless you want to look for another job.' Steinbeck finished.

'Right.' Jack went back to his drawings and in due course the 'thing' emerged new again with a sloping roof.

The engineers looked at it. They weren't particularly enamoured with the slope. They weren't happy, but apparently engineers rarely are. Mr K liked it and therefore it was genius at work. Mr V thought it would add a bit more to the bill which in the scheme of things wasn't anyone's concern except Bill Browns, and he wasn't consulted.

A project manager's job has many and varied tasks. It's a bit like giving a cat a pill, under water. All manner of trades are needed, and all need to be prodded, flattered, cajoled and threatened to get results.

Jack was fresh. He was young. He was what Vern Clutz of Clutz and Sons Builders called a push-over.

Mr Clutz was a man with an opinion on everything. He was more round than tall, with a dirty, greasy hat glued to his head and just enough teeth to chew a plug of tobacco. Mrs Clutz must have seen something in him for he had four sons.

Vern and number one son, Skeet, stood next to their cart and smoked while Bill and Jack stood on the quarter acre. Jack kicked the rock and looked at the strings and pegs vibrating in the wind.

'It'll never do son.' Vern said.

'Never,' Skeet echoed.

Bill paced. He could see the summer slipping away as they stood on his rocks.

'Mr Brown?' Jack felt he should at least give the client a choice, it was his money after all.

'Well...'

'That's igneous ya know.' Vern threw his cigarette end on the ground and thrust his hands into his overall pockets.

'Igneous,' Skeet echoed scratching his head.

'Well...' Bill winced at the thought of abandoning the Parson quarter acre. He'd purchased it for practically a song from ol' Huff Parson. Bill liked to think he got the better of the deal.. Huff Parson was the type of farmer who held onto everything for the day when it might be useful.

'Ya just never know,' was a phrase often heard but never acted upon. Why he buried his old machines was a question often asked. Jack asked as he tripped over a large bit of rusted iron.

'Son, some people don't like to be reminded of their mistakes.' Vern said.

They all looked at the pegs denoting Torheit's perimeter.

'Oh.' Jack coughed and looked at his shoes.

Bill put his hands in his pocket and rested his foot on a lump of rusting machinery.

'Whatever it takes.' he kicked rusting hulk.

'Icon Mr Brown. It will be an icon,' Jack said. Bill felt he might choke on the word if he said it.

Whatever it takes. Well it would take Mr Clutz quite a few sticks of dynamite.

'Should take three I reckon.' Vern said. 'per hole.'

'Per hole.' Skeet echoed.

'Well what about over there,' Bill pointed a little way down the slope.

'Four.'

'Four.'

It was a big rock. Mr Clutz looked over the rock. He made a few exploratory holes.

There is an art to setting dynamite. Vern was

more your 'put some down a hole and see what happens' type of man.

'Well, the ways I reckons it, we just move this sucker.'

'Sucker.' Skeet grinned.

The sticks of dynamite was put around the rock. BOOM.

There was a shower of dirt, but the rock was still there.

They poked a stick under. BOOM

The dirt was splattered over Bill and his buggy. The horse was none too happy either.

'On top Skeet.' They drilled a hole in the top of the rock which took more than a good hour, three cigarette breaks and a few choice swear words. Vern Clutz twisted his tongue around his teeth and spat.

'A big one son.'

'Big,' Skeet nodded and trotted to the cart. He found the big one.

'Only got one of these little beauties. Should do the trick I reckon. Vern weighed up the stick of dynamite in his hand.

'Do the trick,' Skeet grinned.

KaBOOM.

The blast was enough to flatten Skeet's wingnut ears to his head. They popped right back out in about a minute.

When the dust settled they all looked at the rock. There was a chink, which looked like an outhouse seat on the rock face.

Jack, Bill and Skeet looked at Clutz.

'Reckon we'll dig the beggar out.'

'Dig.' Skeet said.

'Tomorrow.'

'Tomorrow.'

'Will ya be wantin' the rubble?' Vern kicked the stone that had scattered.

'Will I?' Bill asked Jack.

'I did have the idea we'd use it in the footings.'

'Not possible son. Unless you want me to grade it, sort it and such.'

'Sort it.' Skeet nodded.

Jack's education was in the rarefied atmosphere of the lecture hall. Footings were a thing discussed, looked at on slides and calculated with a slide rule. No-one actually got dirty.

Bill looked at the rubble. He figured every little stone cost money. It might just be rubble, but it was his rubble.

'I'll keep them. Put them over there.' Bill pointed.

'Are ya sure now. I could get something for em' if ya want. Not much mind, but I know a fella.'

'Know a fella.'

Imagine recouping some money. It sounded like sound economic sense. Farmers are renowned for sound economic sense—just don't mention beans...

'Alright then.' Bill said.

'This'll be by the hour job Bill. I'm doing ya a favour on this one.'

Bill nodded. It sounded like a deal, a bargain, a favour.

The rest of the afternoon was spent collecting rocks and putting them in the Clutz old cart. What Brown didn't know wouldn't hurt him.

If you added up the hour or two collecting rubble, the time for the trip to the dealer in rubble, the miniscule cut Bill Brown would receive for his rubble, he only lost about $10 on the deal. A bargain!

Although Jack thought Project Manager an advancement in his burgeoning career, he longed to get back to the city. The end of the month was fast approaching and he was looking forward to his little envelope of charity from Mr V. And there were his prospects with Miss Hazel Brown. They say absence makes the heart grow fonder, but that assumed the person with the heart knows the other is alive.

He had the naïve idea that Mr Clutz knew what he was doing. He figured he could flit down to the quarter acre once a week and check on progress. Apparently there is one born every minute...or so Mr Clutz thought.

Jack gave the plans of Torheit to Vern Clutz, pointed out the necessary bits and bobs, talked about scantlings, joists and battens. Mr Clutz nodded and spat.

'Son, don't you worry about nuthin'.'

'Nuthin.'

'In a week ya won't know this place.'

'A week.'

Jack left for the city a smile on his face. Everything was under control. Mr Brown was happy. Mrs Brown plied him with home-made produce and a sweater for Hazel and wished him well.

As Jack waited for a lift to the rail head Douglas

Brown came into the farm yard on a Harley Davidson motorbike. He hopped off and cut the engine.

'That's a mighty fine machine,' Jack walked around the bike.

'Ain't she a beaut.' Douglas smiled. 'Be needin' an automobile soon, wife's not keen with a little 'un on the way.'

'Really.'

'Yup. Father said he'd give me a horse to sell. Should get me started.'

'So you're selling the bike.'

'Yup.'

'How much?'

Jack watched the countryside whiz past as he rattled down the road. He caught a few bugs in his teeth, but it was a small price to pay for the freedom to go when and where one wanted. He just hoped his pay packet would cover the first of many instalments to Douglas Brown.

The apprentices came to admire the bike.

'Nice,' Swindon said.

Putney whistled. 'Sweet.'

'Bet she goes,' Steinbeck said walking around the bike.

'Mr Renfrew, boy racer.' Huxley slapped Jack on the back. 'And how was the country?'

Jack sat at his table and described the country. As he was in such a good mood, his description was full of poetry, the flowers, the trees, the sky and the rocks.

It all sounded a bit too idyllic.

'And the build?' Swindon asked.

'Yes, what about Torheit?' Steinbeck added.

'Well...its early days. There is quite a bit of rock on the site.'

'Ah.' Putney nodded.

The apprentices hung off Jack's every word as if waifs in the workhouse who never see the sun.

'Well, you still have your hair, so that's a good sign.' Steinbeck said.

Jack ran his fingers through his hair. He couldn't quite see what all the fuss was about. Edgar must have been a nervous type of fellow. Someone to whom delegation didn't come easily. That could be the only explanation, because the job of Project Manager didn't seem that hard. All one needed to do was work with the builder, the client, and the firm. If everyone co-operated, then it was easy. Jack sat back and thought on where he might go first on his motorbike. The obvious choice was Aunt Jane's residence to deliver the sweater. Mothers know a thing or two about getting people together. He had supplanted himself into the Browns and Mrs Parker was more than a client, she was family. He was day dreaming when Arlan, the mailroom boy poked his head around the corner of the door jam. He whistled.

'He wants ya.'

'That your motorbike outside?'

'Yes,' Jack smiled.

Arlan let out a long whistle. 'Lucky.'

'Yes.' Jack thought it was the perfect name for his Harley-Davidson. He felt lucky.

'Yes Mr Kartoffelkopf.'

'No, Mr Kartoffelkopf.' Jack tried to remember

how lucky he was. It was a hard job, but not as hard as trying to explain why V & K had several telegrams from Steerforth County Planning Department.

'Do you know this man,' Mr K pointed to the signature of the County Planner, a Mr Freelan Quill.

'No sir.'

'He says 'CEASE WORK STOP VIOLATION STOP' Mr K picked up another telegram 'APPROVAL NEEDED STOP'

'Well?' Mr K gave Jack a withering stare.

'Mr Clutz assured me we had all the paperwork. He said he knew a fella. He said he was on top of it.' Jack swallowed—hard.

'Clutz?'

'Yes sir. The builder sir. Mr Brown said he was recommended.'

'Brown?'

'Yes sir.'

Mr K frowned and looked like he had never heard the name before.

'Mr Brown sir. The client.' Jack said.

'Ah.' Mr K narrowed his eyes.

'the Browns . The man who pays the bills.'

There was an awkward moment as Mr K looked like he was thinking. He snorted air through his rather large nostrils and gritted his teeth.

'Sir?'

'Hmmm?'

'There is a slight problem.'

'A problem ja?'

'Yes sir.' And Jack went on to describe a dirty great big igneous rock that defied their efforts to move it. It was just where Torheit needed to be.

'The engineer said we couldn't move the house,

because of the geological anomalies.'

'Anomalies, ja?'

'Yes, I think he meant the bog.'

'Ah.' Mr K went back to thinking, his nostrils working overtime.

'We were wondering, Mr Brown and I, if we could just work around the boulder somehow. Sort of shorten one side of Torheit, sort of.' Jack tried to smile and not look like an idiot.

'What?'

'Sort of bring one side in a bit. It would only loose three feet or so.'

The nostrils flared. The eyes blazed. Mr K looked like he might explode.

'My work? You want to change my work?'

'It was Mr Clutz's idea really.'

'Ja. An idiot. They breed idiots in the country, ja?'

'Sir.'

'Ja?'

'Sir, have you ever been to the country? Jack felt Mr K was going too far. He felt he needed to defend his country folk.

'Where is it?'

'The country. Where honest decent folks live.' Jack felt his blood boiling.

'These people are philistines, barbarians, boors.'

'They may well be sir, but they are,' Jack hunted for the overused phrase, 'the salt of the earth.'

'HA.' Mr K threw his cape over his shoulders, struck a pose and grabbing his hat, strode out of the room.

Jack stood in the office and did a bit of heavy breathing through his own nostrils. He figured his career was over before it had begun. He had a motorbike to pay for, and his pay envelope was due the next day.

'Damnation.'

'Pardon,' Mac came into the office.

'Excuse me,' Jack blushed.

'Mr K said you should go.'

Jack slumped and sighed.

'Immediately,' Mac added.

The thought of losing his pay packet fell like a sword (probably that fellow Damocles) in his chest.

'Do you think if I said something,' Jack began.

'Pardon?' Mac frowned.

'Apologised perhaps.'

'For what? I don't follow you?'

'I was curt with Mr K. I forgot to be invisible.'

'Mr Renfrew. I don't know what you're on about, but you need to get down to Steerforth County right away and get this thing sorted. On the quiet, Mr K said he was hoping for the Bossart Award of Excellence for Torheit. He's counting on you.'

'Me?' Jack squeaked.

'Yes, you.' Mac poked him in the chest with her pencil. She pulled Jack out of the office and made him wait.

'Here,' she handed him an envelope. As you will be away tomorrow, I'll give it to you now. Mr V does them early so he can have the day free.'

'My pay?'

'Of course silly. Now you need to skedaddle. I will mark you away for the week. You need to find somewhere to stay. We will want letters, telegrams if urgent. I don't suppose they have a telephone at the Browns.'

'No. Not even electricity.'

'So letters and telegrams it is.' Mac wrote it down.

'Thanks Mac.

'Take the rest of the day to get organised. I'll send one of the apprentices down during the week for a report.'

'OK.'

'I'll send a telegram to Mr Freelan Quill, let him know you're coming.'

'Right.'

'Remember, here we make man to our own designs.' Mac held her finger in the air.

They laughed, although Jack felt he'd been put through the wringer and come out like a German pretzel.

Back in the dungeon he explained his position. The apprentices listened and nodded.

'And I received this,' Jack held his pay envelope aloft.

'Miracles do happen.' Huxley said.

'Welcome aboard Renfrew,' Putney slapped Jack on the back.

'Looks like you're here to stay,' Steinbeck said.

'Nice to have you as one of us,' Swindon added.

'Thanks.'

Perhaps, Jack thought, it was his lucky day.

With just an afternoon to pack, organise his rent with Mrs Makowski and try to fit all he needed on the motorbike, it was early evening when he finally knocked on Mrs Parker's front door.

'You,' Clarissa said. 'Come in.'

'Ah, you.' Aunt Jane said from a wingback chair near the window.

'Mrs Parker.' Jack smiled. He had the distinct feeling his visit was unwelcome with the frosty reception. He'd thought of himself as practically family, and now...

'My niece is out, Mr Renfrew. A Miss Porter I think, taking her life into her own hands.'

'Pardon?'

'Lessons Mr Renfrew. Miss Porter is a pupil.'

'Oh, I see.

'Are you staying for tea?'

'Well...' Jack didn't want to linger in the room full of curios longer than necessary. It was unnerving to have a shrunken head staring at you.

'Hazel won't be long.'

Jack looked at his watch. He still had his washing to do and find a way to pack his theodolite.

'Sit.'

'Yes Ma'am.' Jack sat. 'Er, Mrs Brown sent this,' he held out the package containing the sweater, 'for Miss Brown.'

'Set it there,' Aunt Jane said. They looked at one another. Aunt Jane smiled. Jack smiled back and looked at his watch.

'I really should go Mrs Parker. I only came by to say I'd be away for a week.'

'A week?'

'Yes. A week.'

'A week is a long time my boy.' Aunt Jane gave a knowing wink. Jack missed the nuance completely. For some reason he had the idea Miss Hazel Brown hung off his every word and was dazzled by just being near him. He thought she, like Helen of Troy, might be hanging about waiting for him to whisk her away.

'Work I'm afraid.' Jack puffed out his chest. 'I'm project manager.'

'Ah work.' Aunt Jane closed the book in her lap.

'Yes. I'm working on Torheit. That's Mr and Mrs Brown's home. Miss Brown's parents.'

'I think I know who they are my boy.'

'Yes of course.' Jack looked at his watch. All he could see was that shrunken head scoffing at his discomfort.

Aunt Jane gave the impression she was reading his mind and analysing his innards.

'We are getting a telephone,' Aunt Jane said.

'Oh.' Jack wondered if Mrs Parker had a touch of the sun.

'People can ring us any time.'

'Yes, that's the idea.' Jack started to fidget on the chair.

'Anyone at all can ring if they know our number.'

'So I've heard.' The woman was barking mad. Jack hoped it didn't run in the family.

'Would you like our number Mr Renfrew?'

Most men would jump at the chance to ring the young lady who was purported to hang off their every utterance. Most men would see it as a distinct advantage to keep in contact with a young lady.

Jack missed the hint. It went so fast over his head it took his hat off.

'Excuse me Mrs Parker, I've got to go,' Jack sprang up from his chair like he'd found a hot poker in his trousers and made for the door.

'Good afternoon Mr Renfrew.'

'Good afternoon, Mrs Parker.' He flew out of the house as if his trousers were on fire.

Three hours on a motorbike gives a fellow time to think. Jack did a lot of thinking.

By the time he arrived in Steerforth County he had convinced himself he was the biggest idiot this side of the Mason Dixon line. After his meeting with the Steerforth County Planning Officer he wasn't the only one.

CHAPTER 13

Mr Freelan Quill was a man without a chin. His beady button eyes looked at the world and didn't much like what they saw.

He was a stickler—for just about everything. If the instructions said rub the ointment vigorously into the scalp for hair growth stimulation for eight minutes, he rubbed for no more no less than eight minutes. If a building was to be built in Steerforth County it needed *all* the paperwork signed, sealed and delivered – on time. The words shilly-shally, dither and flim-flam were not in his vocabulary. Any excuse was no excuse. Mr Quill's life was one of order over chaos. And it might have remained so, except for a builder called Vernon Clutz.

If Mr Clutz had a hand in it, Freelan Quill wanted to know who, what, when, where and why. Freelan kept a close eye—a beady eye— on Vernon Clutz & sons.

So, it was no surprise when he found the Clutz hand all over the profoundly inadequate and downright shonky application for a house on the Huff Parson quarter acre recently acquired by Bill Brown. And it didn't take 'Mr Stickler for order over chaos' to see the application as fiction rather than fact.

It was as if the application for a house, (if you could call an apple crate a house), designed by V & K meant diddly-squat. Mr Quill had heard of V & K. He was a well-read stickler, but he was not to be swayed by high falutin' architects. For Quill was fair, no matter how much money was changing hands, (fairness an anomaly in County departments where money is concerned).

If Vernon Clutz thought he could just ride rough shod over procedure, he hadn't got up as early as Freelan Quill, not nearly early enough.

Throwing caution to the wind, Freelan sent a telegram to V & K. Then another, and yet another. He might have telephoned V & K, but balked at the idea. His voice, although his mother thought suited to the choir, wasn't ideal for the telephone, having a rather high pitch and always sounding like a whingy kid. (Some people recognise their limitations).

Now, Freelan sat in his upright chair, behind his tidy desk and pondered the application set before him. The apple crate would require electricity and although the Mayor in his election speech had promised electrification to the county, he had his fingers crossed when he said it. It would require poles, wires, infrastructure which the meagre budget of Steerforth County didn't have or were not likely to get any time soon. The apple crate was set in a hill. There was a code for dwellings dug into the ground. This 'house' didn't follow the code and lastly Clutz had specified domestic dwelling knowing that designation attracts less tax than commercial premises. Surely it was a gross mistake. No-one could live in an apple crate.

Mr Quill tapped his pencil on his front teeth. There was something more going on and Freelan Quill was the man to find out.

Mac had specified Jack should find digs in Brownsville and V & K would remit the rent. He went to the post office and asked. The directions were written down and after a false start he rode up to a small wooden cottage with a delightful garden and sunny porch.

Mrs Sweetwater stood at the door and looked Jack over. He picked a grasshopper from his chin strap and smiled.

'Mrs Sweetwater?'

'Yes.'

'I was told you have a room for rent, by the week.'

'Yes.'

'I was wondering if a room is available.' Jack kept smiling at the old woman. She was entirely in black, about four foot tall and looked whip smart.

'Come, look.' Mrs Sweetwater led the way down a dark corridor that divided the house. The walls were decorated with family photographs, lots of them.

The room was small, but homely. It was more

than he'd had on the farm as a boy.

'I'll take it.'

'You want to know the price.'

'Oh, sorry. Yes.'

With the transaction completed, Jack unpacked his small valise and sat on the bed. The room had a crucifix on the wall, a wash basin stand and a small wardrobe.

'Tea?' Mrs Sweetwater tapped lightly on Jack's door.

'Yes, please.'

He felt lucky, albeit still the stupidest person this side of the Mason Dixon line, but lucky none-the-less.

Mrs Clara Sweetwater

Mrs Clara Sweetwater was a widow of many years. She was, Jack thought, just about the sweetest old woman he'd met.

He sat at the kitchen table and ate several home baked biscuits and sipped his tea. Mrs Sweetwater watched him and urged him to take another biscuit.

'Thank you.'

'Mr Sweetwater, he liked these. He died right in that room.' Clara pointed down the passage to the back of the house. Jack hoped there was another bed somewhere, rather than the one he would be sleeping in.

Yes, Mr Sweetwater liked his food.'

'Yes, I can see why.' Jack said wiping his mouth with a napkin.

'Will you want your evening meal Mr Renfrew?'

'If it's no trouble Mrs Sweetwater.' Jack imagined heaps of meat and vegetables, puddings and custard.

'I'll need to charge you a bit extra.'

'That's alright.' Jack smiled and put his empty plate on the draining board.

'Have you lived here in Brownsville all your life Mrs Sweetwater?' Jack sat back and basked in his good luck.

'Oh I think so. Mr Sweetwater was from Briskitt Bridge, just a mile away, so I think you could say we are from these parts. I had my five girls right here in Brownsville.'

'Really.'

'Oh yes. Enid, she's the eldest. Rose, Elenora, Faith and Charity. All married now and families of their own. I have thirty five grandchildren and eleven great grandchildren. Enid has ten you know.'

'Ten.' Jack thought women quite amazing.

'We had a bit of bother not long gone. My grand-daughter got stood up, right at the altar. What a to-do.'

'I should say so.'

Clara Sweetwater liked to chatter. She would lure the unsuspecting into her kitchen, plie them with cake and bend their ear.

'They all live right here in Brownsville. Well on a farm, but close enough.'

'Fancy.'

'Enid and William are taking it easy now. Douglas and Beth are taking over the farm. She's got a little 'un due any day now.'

'Yes, farming is hard work.' Jack said, although as he sat at the kitchen table, not a beet in sight, he looked on farming as something a little more poetic than grubbing out weeds, watching the weather, worrying about the prices and the bank loan. Jack was in that place where people wear rose coloured glasses and go around with a smile on their face.

'Enid says they are building something nice. For their 'take it easy' times. Something with all those catalogue things you read about.'

'That's nice.' Jack thought on his 'take it easy' times in the future. Sitting on a porch, much like Mrs Sweetwater's. Biscuits, much like Mrs Sweetwater's. A large family to look back on, much like Mrs Sweetwater's.

While he was dreaming the connection of Mrs Sweetwater and the Browns went in one ear and out the other.

You might be on the money to say he was the

biggest idiot this side, and the other side, of the Mason Dixon line.

With an evening to himself Jack went for a stroll before his dinner. Brownsville wasn't your den of iniquity on a Monday evening. It wasn't humming with people on their way to find a good time. Most of its inhabitants were indoors minding their own (and other peoples') business.

Jack found a lone dog to pat to convince himself he was full of kindness for dumb animals. After a lap around the town square a look at the county office, an inspection of the library times and a thorough read of the bulletin board extolling the virtues of Gunther's chickens, the merits of an old sofa for sale or swap and the postponement of the knitting circle due to family matters – the next one held at Mrs Delany's on the 16th, he headed back to the expected wonderful home cooking. Mrs Sweetwater heard the door.

'Just in time.'

Over a homecooked meal Jack heard all about Mrs Delany and her family matter. It involved a kidney complaint, a wayward son and a long standing feud with Cora O'shea.

'More Mr Renfrew?'

'That would be lovely Mrs Sweetwater. The custard was accompanied by the story of Clem Frankston and his prize winning bull. Jack lapped it up.

'I'm here to see the County planning officer. A Mr Freelan Quill.'

Mrs Sweetwater put the kettle on and drew breath. Jack listened as Freelan's life history was given the once over.

'Really?'

'Oh yes.'

'Fancy that.'

'Exactly what Mrs Delany said.'

'My word.'

'I thought of a few Mr Renfrew.' Clara Sweetwater said. 'Quite a few. Now, don't you let Freelan boss you around.'

'No, I won't.'

Mrs Sweetwater nodded, 'more tea?'

Breakfast was everything Jack dreamed. He sat and tucked into a hearty meal. A man can achieve anything if he starts the day with a hearty breakfast.

Jack gathered his plans, adjusted his starched collar and after sponging off a little bit of egg on his trousers he was ready to tackle the day.

Freelan Quill started his day with dry toast. He had a delicate constitution, so his mother said. He sipped his tea and tried to enjoy his toast.

At nine o'clock Mr Quill was at his desk, his collar starched and rubbing his shaving rash.

At nine o'clock Jack waited outside the planning office and burped.

'Go right in,' Miss Lillian Delany pointed to the door.

'Thank you Miss.' Jack smiled and Lillian blushed.

The combatants eyed one another.

'Mr Quill.'

'Mr Renfrew.'

Jack held out his hand and Quill took it with a modicum of reluctance. He'd had dealings with wheeler-dealers from the city types and thought he knew their game. Quill narrowed his eyes, 'Sit down Mr Renfrew.'

'Pleasure.' Jack sat and put his hat on his lap then looked up expectantly.

'Now, I understand you are V & K's representative.'

'Yes. Bit of luck really.' Jack smiled and started to relax. This fellow without a chin didn't look like someone who would balk at a clerical error. In fact, he looked harmless—albeit with a touch of indigestion.

'Mr Renfrew, your luck—or otherwise is not why we are here.'

'No, I guess not.'

Quill looked at the clock on the wall.

'Right.' Jack revised his initial assessment. 'Time marches on eh?'

That was another thing Freelan Quill disliked. The use of catchy phrases, catchy tunes, catchy popular anything grated Freelan like fingernails on a blackboard.

He winced. 'Quite.'

'Well,' Jack sat forward. 'I'm sure we can fix this in two shakes of a lambs tail.'

Freelan pursed his lips and grimaced.

'Mr Clutz submitted the paperwork. Must have missed something. A dotted i or a crossed t.' Jack gave a carefree giggle. Freelan looked like he was sitting with a 2 by 4 splintered plank up his back. 'Have it fixed in a jiffy.' Jack smiled and nodded.

'We'll see about that Mr Renfrew. The feeling of magnanimity flowed over a full breakfast and Jack burped.

'Excuse me. Country hospitality,' he smiled. 'You won't believe the breakfast I had,' and he described the eggs, hash browns, biscuits and gravy, sausages, toast, marmalade 'which was homemade Mr Quill. Delicious.' Jack licked his lips. 'Can't beat ma's home cooking.' He sang the catchy popular jingle for Ma's fruit conserve, 'straight from the farm to table.'

Freelan curled his toes in his polished shoes.

'Mr Renfrew. You don't necessarily realise that procedure, order, and paperwork needs to be followed to a satisfactory conclusion.' Freelan voice went up an octave, if such a thing were possible for a grown man. He sounded whingy, whiny and petulant.

'That's why I'm here Mr Quill.'

'If I could draw your attention to this application. Mr Clutz suggests in a moment of fancy that this 'Torheit', this structure will be a dwelling.'

'Yes.'

'A house.'

'Yes.'

'A place where people reside.'

'The Browns. Yes.'

'You are telling me that this...' and here Freelan pointed to the drawing Huxley had rendered with about a dozen urns scattered here and there, 'is a home?'

'Yes.'

Where do you take the conversation from there?
'For the Browns?'
'Yes.'
Freelan took another look at the apple crate.
He turned it upside down. Jack leaned forward and
turned it back. He looked at Freelan and imagined
him in Sunday School with his hair plastered to his
head. He saw Freelan as the weedy boy afraid of
catching the ball, the spindly youth, afraid of girls,
the young man afraid of bacon and hash browns. He
looked at Freelan's bitten fingernails. Jack thought
he had Freelan Quill pretty well pegged.

'Well. Never-the-less it needs to comply.'

'With...?'

'It is built into the ground. There are rules.
Standards.'

'I think you will find Mr Quill that Torheit while
looking like its snuggled into a hill, is actually on
the hill A clever use of cantilever. A sort of trick of
the eye. You do know what a cantilever is?' Jack
opened a schematic diagram, 'Autochthonous.' The
big word came in handy now and again. Quill was
losing 2-0.

'Well, what about this?' He pointed to a diagram
of the electricity.

'Ah.' Jack looked at the finger on the plan,
noting the bitten fingernail.

'Ah ha!' Quill thought he'd pulled back a point
on the score.

'I've had a chat with the electrical company,'
Jack peered at the diagram, 'and Mr Clutz regarding
the lines, the poles etc,' Jack waved his hand in the
air to extrapolate the etc 'and I find the poles, the
lines etc are all in the modernisation plans for the

county. I think you will find they are laying lines as we speak.

The score was 3 –0.

What Freelan Quill didn't' know, couldn't know, and would find out in due course, was the Mayor's plan for a golf course down past the Huff Parson quarter acre and that it would require electricity for its facilities. Thing like an electric lights for dances and its ball polishers which were found in the Blathers & Roundtree Golfing catalogue.

Mayors can get things done when the need arose. No need for any of that planning permission folderol. Captains of industry in the county required a golf course and the Mayor was just the man to give it to them.

'By God, I'll do it,' was the Mayor's catchphrase which got him elected and now got him a golf course.

Quill drew himself up in his chair, 'That may well be the case Mr Renfrew. The electrification company hasn't informed my department.'

'I can't answer for your department Mr Quill.'

That got Freelan's dander up. He took pride in knowing what was happening and to whom.

'Well...Mr Clutz forgot to date this,' Freelan was clutching at straws. Jack took the paper and dated it, added his signature and slid it back.

'You know Mr Quill, Torheit by V & K will be the chance to put Steerforth County on the map.'

'We are on the map Mr Renfrew.' Freelan's dander turned sour.

'Heck, to preside over an icon in the district.

That's worth something isn't it?' The word icon caught in Freelan's throat. He didn't care for the aggrandisement of Mr Renfrew and his icon. Not one bit.

'I am in this position as Steerforth County Planning Officer to make sure anything that is built in this County is regulated. Icon or no icon.'

'And doing a fine job too Mr Quill. Now, if there is nothing else?' Jack gathered his plans. A full country breakfast beats a dry bit of toast any day of the week.

'I will be watching you and your icon Mr Renfrew. I will be watching very closely.'

'You do that Mr Quill.'

'And I will be watching Vernon Clutz.'

'I'm sure he will appreciate an audience Mr Quill. As the name Clutz will forever be associated with an icon and probably no-one will hear the name Quill.'

That stung. Well, a full breakfast or not, magnanimity only stretches so far. Jack stood and walked out the door.

'Icon. Pfft.' Freelan Quill bit his last fingernail down to the quick.

Mr Clutz and number two son, Winslow were smoking sitting on the rock that defied dynamite They watched Jack ride up to the site. They studied his motorbike. They stared at his jacket, his goggles and his cap on backwards.

'How do Mr Clutz.'

'Howdy.' Clutz nodded and winked at Winslow.

'Er, Mr Clutz,'

'Yeah?' It was said with a slow drawl and a spit.

Jack fiddled with his goggles. 'Er, I thought there might be footings.' Jack looked at the unbroken ground. Only the pegs and the string moved. Clutz and son sat.

'Footin's eh?'

'Yes. You see, I have arranged for Zennith Union Electrification company to come and lay a line.'

Vern Clutz studied Jack. It was quite un-nerving.

'Well son, it's like this.' Vern took off his hat and scratched his head. Winslow took up the story. He explained the situation.

'The dray was broke. The shovels was on the dray. The dray was gunna get a new wheel, but Clem, he says the job was off, 'till Monday. Clem says he's doin' sommit else.'

'So, that's about the size of it.' Vern threw his cigarette end on the ground.

'So, how did you get here?' Jack looked around for a vehicle, a horse, a bicycle.

'Skeet brung us.' Winslow said.

'Brought,' Jack corrected. The grammatical went right over Winslow's head.

'Well, why can't Skeet get the shovels?' It seemed so obvious to Jack. The Clutz clan looked at Jack as if he had suggested they forget building and plumb for the Nobel Prize instead.

'Skeet's not 'ere.' Winslow looked at Jack as if he was a bit thick between the ears.

'I can see that.'

'So that's about the size of it.' Vern offered his homily as an end to silly suggestions. Jack paced in front of the men, thinking.

'Where is the dray? I'll get the shovels.'

'You?'

'Yes.'

'On that?'

'Yes.'

'Now son. I don't know much, but we're not doing any double handling.'

'Pardon.'

'We get the shovels an' where do we put the spoil?'

'On the ground?'

'And then when we git the dray we got ta shovel it in the dray'

'Double handlin',' Winslow said and nodded.

'An' my time ain't free,' Vern added.

'No.' Jack felt a sickening feeling he was losing the argument.

'An' double handlin', well that...' Vern didn't need to go on.

'Monday you said?' Jack kicked the dirt.

'There 'bouts.'

There was a moment of quiet as they contemplated, there 'bouts. It could mean anything. Jack took a deep breath. He squared his shoulders and turned his back on the men for a moment and silently screamed into the wind. After his cathartic scream he turned back and repositioned his cap.

'So, what are you doing now Mr Clutz?'

'Figurin'.'

'What?'

'Figurin' this 'ere Tor-hight.'

'Torheit,' Jack corrected.

'More like Jim Dandy's apples.' Vern said which made Winslow laugh.

'Look son. I'll be wantin' lumber, cement, nails.'

'Have you ordered lumber Mr Clutz?'

'Still figurin' son. I know a fella. He owes me a favour.' Winslow grinned.

'As much lumber as a fella needs.'

'I see.' Jack took a deep breath of the bracing country air. He needed all the oxygen he could get.

'Skeet'll be by directly. Now don't you go worryin' about this Jim Dandy house.' Vern stood up and spat. 'She'll get done.'

Jack looked to the sky.

'Weather'll hold son.'

'So what are you doing here now Mr Clutz?'

'Well, we're gettin' paid to be here.'

'Yes.'

'So we're here ain't we.'

'Well, yes. But couldn't you be somewhere doing something?'

'I'd hate to rob ol' Bill Brown. He's paying for us to be here.'

'Right. But you don't seem to be doing anything.'

'Ever built a house son?'

'Well, no. But...'

'Just leave it to me son.'

'Yes,' Jack took a dejected look at the boulder.

'Any chance?'

'Not a hope in hell, 'xcuse the expression.' Vern said. Winslow stood up and kicked the rock.

'Ain't a hope in hell,' he said.

A project manager could yell, pull his hair out, threaten and make a scene, but Jack talked himself out of all four actions. He took a breath. These things happen, he said to himself. Things are bound to happen that are out of one's control.

'I guess it's just one of those things,' he said. This would be another one of those underrated and overused phrases that cover a multitude of situations. Sort of a one size fits all, get out of gaol phrases. Jack stored it away for further use, he had a feeling he would need it.

'Just as you say. One of those things.' Vern spat and put his hands in his pockets and shrugged.

'Yup.' Winslow sauntered after his father.

With nothing to look at, Jack pondered the boulder. He fetched his plans and put a critical eye to the problem.

'Autochthonous.' The word popped into his head and stayed there. Why not make the rock an integral part of the design. It might be Mr Renfrew's idea, but it would soon be Mr Kartoffelkopf's ingenious genius that would give it life. Authorship is a tricky business when you are an apprenticed to a genius, who is sometimes called a potato-head.

It would be later, much later Mr K's autochthonous would be put to the test. The rock would be part of the fireplace.

'Sort of bring the outside inside, ja?'

V & K had sent Jack to oversee, but as there was nothing to see – over or otherwise, he cast his eye about the countryside. It really was the perfect place to sit and enjoy the rest of your days. He thought he'd quite like something similar when the time came—albeit more conventional.

Mr Brown drove up in his horse and buggy and waved to Jack.

'Someone said they saw Dougie's motorbike

with a fella on it. Thought it might-a been you.'

Jack nodded. Nothing gets past the lace curtain brigade in a small country town.

Mr Brown continued. There was the errand into Brownsville. The shopping for a bath plug, 'they're an extra ya know.' Then the chance meeting with Mrs Delany. The information she passed on was mulled over. Mrs Delany got it from Gertrude who heard it from Mrs Quill.

Jack nodded.

'So I figured it'd be you.'

'Amazing.'

'Isn't it.' Bill drew breath and looked over the site. He frowned. Jack saw the disconcerted look and stepped up.

There was the ride from the city, the meeting at the county planning office, the estimation of Mr Quill's worth in doing his job, then the points scoring of Mr Quill. Then the news from Mr Clutz, the timeline of Clem and his wheel and lastly the weather.

Bill looked at the Clutz clan.

'He's figuring.' Jack said.

'Son, if there is one thing I know about Vern Clutz, he's figuring how to get a bigger cut.'

'Oh.'

'Now you just send him over here and I'll get this thing sorted. Vern Clutz and me go way back. He's a good builder, none finer, you just need to know how to handle him.'

'Right.'

'Er, Mr Clutz, Mr Brown would like a word.'

'Does he now?' Clutz spat and sauntered over to Bill in his buggy.

Jack went to his motorbike and fiddled with some straps and tried to eavesdrop. He watched the men shake hands after a protracted conversation. Mr Clutz stood back and Brown turned his buggy around and off the site. He beckoned Jack over.

'Follow me.'

'Now?'

'Yep.'

Bill took hold of the reins and drove back to the farm, Jack right behind.

'What did you say, Mr Brown?' Jack thought he'd heard wrong.

'I'm giving him a hog.'

'A hog?'

'That's right. If Clem will butcher it, he can have a hind. Then the dray can get fixed and Vern can start a-diggin'.'

'I'm not quite sure I understand?' Jack shook his head to clear his thoughts. All of a sudden a pig was vital to getting a house built.

'It's like this,' And once again there was the matter of the outstanding debt from Skeet Clutz to Clem's son, Harlan who was a farrier. The debt was carried over to Vern and so Clem was keeping him waiting. 'Horse shoes don't grow on trees you know!'

'Right.' Jack was still following.

'So...' Bill went on. That ol' dray wasn't likely to get fixed any time soon...unless there was a pig involved.

'I thought Mr Clutz said Clem was busy.'

'There's busy and there's busy son. Clem is the slaughterman as well as the wheelwright.'

'I'm not quite following you Mr Brown.'

'Right. I give a hog to Vern. He pays Clem who butchers it, keeps some as payment, fixes the wheel. Clutz starts diggin' while Mrs Clutz make the most of the hog.

If you don't grow up in the country it can be hard to see how things operate. Jack, although a country boy, knew for a fact no-one wanted beets, no-one traded for beets and no-one thought beets a good bargain.

If every job was going to require a pig, a bushel of gooseberries or a few jars of homemade pickles Jack thought he was in the wrong profession.

'Do you see now son?'

'Yes, but should you really pay a hog for your footings? Mr Clutz put his tender in and...' Bill held up his hand.

'Son, listen.' And then he heard about the long standing dispute between Mrs Clutz and Mrs Brown over the Steerforth County Fair potted meat prize.

'Sally Clutz will be using our hog for the fair. Mrs Brown will have something to crow about.

'Potted meat.' Jack frowned.

'Son, if there is one thing I've learnt in all my years, it's keep the wife happy.'

'Happy.' Jack was beginning to sound like Skeet Clutz.

'Yes sirreee. Happy. A hog might not be the sweetest smelling, but this hog will go on smelling sweet for a long time to come.

'I get my footings. Mrs Brown gets her blue ribbon. Clem knows where the hog came from and that's all there is to it.' Bill smiled and looked up to see Enid come out of the house. She wiped her hands on her apron, fixed her hair and asked, 'you staying here Mr Renfrew?'

'Well,' Jack began, 'I don't want to impose. I'm renting a room. In town.'

'Nonsense. You bring your things right over.'

'Now Edie,' Bill said, 'if a fella wants to be in town, he's got every right.' Bill winked at Jack.

'Well...have something to eat. Lunch is ready.'

'I couldn't really.'

'Get inside and wash up.'

'Mr Brown likes a hot lunch,' Enid set a full plate of meat pie and vegetables in front of Jack. He was still surviving quite well on his breakfast. He groaned as he picked up his knife and fork.

'Eat.' Mrs Brown had spoken.

The last thing Jack saw as he left the Brown farm was a hog in the back of the buggy. Just the thought of potted meat made Jack burp.

He rode the Harley Davidson back to Brownsville and pulled up at his digs.

'Just in time,' Mrs Sweetwater said from the front door.

'Get inside and wash up.'

'Mrs Sweetwater, I didn't expect...'

'Mr Sweetwater always liked a hot lunch.'

'Oh.'

Jack sat at the table and was given a large helping of rib roast. He groaned.

'Eat.'

Something sounded quite familiar.

Country hospitality can be downright painful.

Jack felt his stomach was at its absolute maximum.

'I think I'll just lie down for a minute.

The minute turned into a few hours and Jack finally woke to a setting sun and the sound of Mrs Sweetwater clattering in the kitchen. If he had any hope of surviving he needed to get out before the dinner table was set.

'Just going out. I won't be back for dinner Mrs Sweetwater.'

'I'll leave something on the sideboard, just in case.'

'Thank you.' Jack almost ran out the door.

Brownsville still didn't have a night life. He patted the same dog, walked the same streets and looked at the same notice board. Apparently the sofa had been purchased, but a chicken coop was on offer. As he sat and pondered the events his mind came back to a pig, potted meat and a debt. The young man felt he should be doing something more for his wage than eating his own weight in country hospitality. This wasn't what he had in mind. V & K were a professional outfit. Mr K was practically a genius and Mr V would want to know how their money was being spent. A good strong talking to oneself can work wonders. Jack loosened his belt and decided things were going to be done in a professional manner. Mr Clutz would need to get organised. Just because his dray was out of order was no excuse. Just because Skeet owed money was nothing to do with Torheit. There needed to be a line drawn between professional and private. There needed to be some sort of understanding.

First thing in the morning he would crack the whip. There was a schedule to adhere to, an estimate to consider and a job to be done. Jack Renfrew felt he was the man to do it. The thought gave him a backbone. He flexed it. He was the project manager. That should count for something.

CHAPTER 14

'Well, these things happen,' Jack said as the men looked at the rain and sheltered under a hastily erected canvas awning.

The water cascaded down the site and formed little rivulets which turned into bigger rivulets which ended in the bog, which resembled a lake, albeit a small one.

'Not unusual.' Vern looked at the sky.

'Unusual,' Skeet said.

Bill Brown drew his buggy up next to the makeshift awning. He pulled on his hat and readjusted his raincoat. The horse stomped and snorted as it stood in the rain.

'Any chance?'

Jack looked at Vern. Vern spat on the ground and moved the plug of tobacco to the other cheek.

'Not looking good Bill.'

'Er Mr Brown, if I could have a word?'

Jack climbed up on the buggy and Bill gave him an old oilskin tarp for shelter.

'I need to send a report to V & K and as yet nothing has happened. I wonder if I should, I mean ..well you know...just get things moving.'

'Moving eh?'

'Yes.' Jack wanted to say crack the whip, but thought better of it.

'Did the hog...?'

'It did. Clem's on the wheel as we speak. That's why I came out.'

'Oh, that's grand.' Jack was feeling better by the minute.

'I'll take Vern back to get his dray. First sign of better weather and...'

'Footings,' Jack said. They looked at the Clutz clan smoking under their awning while their nag stood in the rain.

'Er Mr Clutz,' Jack beckoned. Vern listened and it began to dawn on him that the sun would come out and he'd need to work for a living. It wasn't a pleasant thought, but Vern Clutz liked to eat like the rest of the population.

The woman behind the counter at the telegraph office read back the note.

WORK PROCEEDING STOP SCHEDULE ONE DAY BEHIND STOP WEATHER HOLDUP STOP RENFREW

'Yes, that's all.' Jack sent it collect. He went to the stationers and purchased a card.

Dear Miss Brown,

Sorry I missed you. When you write I will be at Mrs Sweetwater's residence, third Street Brownsville for the week. Mrs S-Water doesn't have a telephone, so you cannot call me. your friend, Jack Renfrew.

The letter hit all the right spots, Jack thought. Although he'd had an epiphany in regard to being an idiot, he still nursed the idea Hazel Brown was waiting with baited breath.

His letter, albeit grammatically correct, would hit a spot alright. No-one likes to be told what to do, especially young entrepreneurs, young woman entrepreneurs in particular.

He posted it to Mrs Parker's and felt things were really getting on track. People can often convince themselves of just about anything with the right motivational spiel. Jack might have been an expert in this regard. He stood outside the post office and looked at the sky. The rain had stopped and the sun was beginning to shine.

Mrs Sweetwater was waiting at the door as Jack rode up to the house.

'Just in time.'

There is nothing more satisfying that a hot lunch after a morning's work. That Jack hadn't actually done any work was neither here nor there. He felt he had cracked the whip, the work was proceeding, his superiors would be happy, Hazel would be happy and Mr and Mrs Brown's icon would rise from the bog. A chicken pie and steamed chocolate pudding can work miracles.

What a chocolate pudding cannot do is make a builder work a bit faster.

Jack rode out to the block after his hot lunch, full of more than pudding. He felt he needed to assert his authority with the builder. He needed to supervise, organise and control the build. He watched from a distance as Vern, Skeet, Winslow and number three son, Woodruff dug and flung the spoil on the dray. They didn't look like they were in any hurry.

Skeet spotted him in the distance and stopped work. The others looked up. Jack waved back and walked to the site.

'Getting on then?'

'Yup.' Winslow said and leaned on his shovel.

'This here is Woodruff,' Vern said.

'Pleased to meet you.' Jack nodded.

'I just wonder...' Jack began and then he made the mistake countless others have made over the years. He was young. He was inexperienced in the ways of tradesmen. He didn't know, but he soon would. 'I just wonder if you moved the dray over there a little and worked in a line, wouldn't it be more efficient?'

Vern looked at the whippersnapper.

'You cut a footing before son?'

'Well, no, but it seems to me...' Tradesmen have an aversion to 'advice'. It's a little like a man telling a woman giving birth isn't so bad.

Winslow stopped working. Woodruff put his shovel down and made a cigarette. This was gonna be good.

Vern handed Jack the shovel. 'There ya go son.'

'Well, I just meant...' Jack said.

'Oh? Meant what?'

'Mr Clutz,'

'Yes?'

'I would never presume to tell you how to do your job.'

'You wouldn't.'

'No.' Jack looked at this watch. 'Will you look at the time. I need to go. I'd like to help, but business you see.' Jack hot footed it to his bike, turned his cap, snapped on his goggles and shot off, the Harley put into top speed all the way back to town. He couldn't be sure, but he thought the Clutz clan were laughing as he sped away.

He was quite correct.

Cement is a tricky thing. It needs a skilled hand to mix, pour and tend until set. Mr Clutz had the knack and guarded his expertise like Mrs Clutz guarded a prize winning recipe for potted meat.

Jack hovered as the pour continued, the Clutz clan moving barrow after barrow to the footings. He wondered on the Mpa of the cement, the ratio of the water to sand to mortar and the co-efficient. All meritorious things he'd learnt at university, but in the field it was a bit different.

Mr Clutz put his finger in the mix and looked at it. He rubbed the wet mixture between his fingers and added a bit of this and a little of that.

'Er Mr Clutz,' Jack began. Winslow held up a hand. Obviously the maestro was at work. Woodruff came back for a mixer load. 'Reckon we'll have enough Pa?'

'Yup.' Mr Clutz was bent over the mixture like

an alchemist.

'Last one Woodruff.'

'Right you are Pa.' The barrow was filled and Woodruff trotted off to the footings.

'Last one?' Jack asked.

'Yup,' Winslow said.

'But what about the south side?'

The Clutz clan stared at Jack as if he'd asked them to lick their shovels clean instead of having a hot lunch.

Skeet and Winslow waited for their Pa to answer.

'Now I don't know much son, but I know a bit about this here cement. Do you know anything about cement?'

'Well, a bit.' Jack held his ground.

'Ah.'

'Ah,' said Skeet.

'Well, ya will know that ya can't crowd cement. Ya got to let cement sort of settle down. Ya know that don't ya?'

'Well, yes.'

'An' if ya crowd cement it won't like it. Ya know that don't ya?'

'Well, yes.'

'So we were figurin', if it's alright with you, that is Mr Renfrew, we was figurin' that we'd just let the cement sit a while, take our hot lunch and then come back. If it's alright with you?'

Winslow and Skeet rolled their cigarettes and looked earnestly at Jack. Woodruff came back and spat.

'Well, I'll leave you to it,' Jack felt like a spare peg. He took a quick tour of the footings and then snapped on his goggles and rode into Brownsville cursing the Clutz clan and their cement. They'd made him feel stupid again and Jack thought, I don't need them to make me feel stupid, I can do it all by myself. It wasn't a sobering thought, but it irked him none-the-less.

'Hey ho Renfrew.' Huxley waved the Harley down.

'Roman?'

'And Hazel.' Huxley pointed to the general store.

'Miss Brown? Here?'

'Well, the girl comes from these regions Renfrew.'

'Yes, I know. But I only sent her a letter yesterday.' All Jack could think of was Miss Brown pining for his company. It was a vision that his ego quite liked and might expand upon at every opportunity.

'And here is the young lady now.' Hazel came out of the store and hefted her parcels in the back of Huxley's automobile

'Mr Renfrew.'

'Miss Brown.'

Obviously, his ego thought, she was overcome with emotion. What sort of emotion might be described in unflattering terms. The word livid came to mind.

'We're here to see the build.' Huxley said to break the tension.

'The build.'

'Torheit.'

'OH, Torheit. The build.' Jack pulled himself to-gether as the frosty reception sent a chill up his back.

'Mr K is on tenterhooks. He's up to his neck

with the Monash house, the estimates, I heard were passed off as fiction by Mr Monash.'

'Oh.' Jack thought of the Clutz clan standing around smoking and spitting.

'Yes, Mr K is thinking of coming down here in the near future.'

'Here?'

'Yes. Brownsville. The country. Hilarious I know, but there you have it. I'm to give a full accounting of the proceedings and rush right back.

'Not staying then?'

'No.' Huxley looked at Hazel, then at Jack, then back to Hazel.

'I'm staying for a few days.' Hazel opened the door and sat in the driving seat.

'Well, we better get cracking. See you back here Renfrew, I'm just dropping Hazel off and then onward and upward to Torheit.'

'Right.' They drove away and Jack wondered what he'd done to elicit the frosty reception. Why was Huxley so familiar with Hazel Brown and how was he going to explain the slow progress?

'Did Miss Brown say why she's here?' Jack asked as they drove to Torheit'

'No.'

'So, Renfrew, how is the country?'

'Muddy.'

The Clutz clan had gone, their horse had left a parting gift and Huxley stepped in it.

'And a bit smelly,' Jack said as Huxley hobbled

over to a tuft of grass and wiped his shoe.

'Mr K has had a few ideas.' Huxley took a rolled plan from his trunk and spread it out on the bonnet of the automobile.

'Cantilever are the oveur of the moment. One must simply have a cantilever somewhere.'

'We have one.'

'Why have one when you can have two.' Huxley pointed to the plans. A balcony now jutted from the north side.

Jack groaned. The footings were calculated for the building and nothing else. Now a balcony would add extra tension.

'Really Roman?' Jack bleated.

'Style is the problem solved. At first one thinks yes, of course how marvellous. Then later, but what does it do? Mr K thought it might solve the 'porch' problem.'

'It adds quite a bit of work.' Jack said. Then there was the matter of Mr Clutz. That was a tricky one.

They heard a horse whinny and Bill pulled up in his buggy.

'Mr Brown, this is Mr Huxley. He's come to see Torheit, and report back to the office.'

'Howdy,' Bill extended his hand.

'Nice to meet you Mr Brown.' Huxley shook hands. 'Er, we have had a think about your porch.'

'Yes?'

Huxley laid out the plans and pointed to the edition. 'A sort of balcony cum porch. What a view.' Huxley said.

Bill considered the porch. It made the apple crate look lopsided.

'It looks lopsided.'

'Does it?' Huxley said.

'Yup.'

'So, that's a no?'

'Yup.' Bill took the plan and brought out his little black book and his stub of a pencil. 'Here, this is what I had in mind. He drew a large line through the plan and added some uprights. 'That's what I had in mind.'

'I see.' Huxley rolled up the plan before Bill could go to town on his vision. The drawing had taken a good two days to execute.

'I'll certainly let Mr Kartoffelkopf know.'

'You do that Mr Huxley.'

'V & K are very accommodating with clients.

'Glad to hear it.' Bill walked over the footings and gave the cement a poke.

'Do you know anything about cement Mr Brown?' Jack asked.

'Nope.'

'Well, you can't crowd cement. You've got to let cement sort of settle down.'

'Is that right.'

'Yes, and if you crowd cement it won't like it.'

'It won't?'

'No.' Jack shook his head. 'so, Mr Clutz will be back later to finish. Then we wait for the cure. Mr Clutz said he's got the lumber. He can start assembling the frames while the cement cures.' That was the plan. It sounded like a good plan. Jack stood back and basked in the glow of Project Manager having everything under control.

'And the bricks?' Bill Brown asked.

'Ah.' Jack sucked in his top lip and frowned.

'Bricks. I think we settled on the buff'.

'Mrs Brown quite liked those brown ones we saw at that fancy house we drove past.'

'The brown ones.'

'Brown for Brown,' Huxley said. Jack gave him a withering stare. Roman wasn't helping matters.

'That's it.' Bill liked the idea. 'Brown for Brown,' he chuckled.

'I'll tell Mr Kartoffelkopf. He had the idea they would be glazed buff coloured.' Huxley winked at Jack. 'Brown.'

Bill walked the perimeter of Torheit and looked up the hill. While he was out of earshot Jack hissed, 'can we acquire brown bricks?'

'Don't know.' Huxley shrugged.

'That's just brilliant Roman. Why encourage the man? I already had the buff on order.'

'Well, you didn't say.' Roman shook his head. 'How was I to know?'

'Can you find out if Schnider Kiln works can change the order. You're going straight back aren't you?'

'Well, yes. I thought I might pop over the way to see an Aunt or two and have a bit of tea, but after that, I'll be driving back.'

'Well, first thing in the morning.'

'Yes, first thing.'

Bill came back to the buggy. He patted his horse and climbed aboard. 'Brown for Brown,' he chuckled again and drove home.

'Why didn't you tell him you'd already ordered buff?' Huxley cleaned his shoe and hopped in the automobile.

The thought hadn't occurred to Jack. He sat in

the passenger seat and cursed his good nature, his manners and his idiocy.

Huxley pulled up at Jack's lodgings. 'I don't know what Mr K will say. He had his heart set on buff you know. Steinbeck did a cracker of a job on the artwork in buff.'

'Roman, you're not making my job any easier. Just ask tomorrow and let me know. I'll tell the telegraph office to keep my correspondence.'

A groan came from Jack. How do you please all the people all the time? If he found the answer to that one, every politician in the land would beat a path to his door.

'Well, you could let Mr Brown know they are all out of Brown. Bad luck and all that. Sunt mala fortuna.' Huxley put his Arrow66 in gear, 'Be seeing you Renfrew.'

Jack knew a lie wasn't the answer. One slip up and he'd be caught. He strolled to the telegraph office and made arrangements, then with nothing better to do, had another look at the notice board, remarked to himself that $2.00 for a box of horseshoes seemed excessive and went to Mrs Sweetwater's for a cup of tea and biscuits.

'I've just put the kettle on,' Mrs Sweetwater said, 'my granddaughter said she'd be visiting.

The thought of trying to make conversation to a snotty nosed child wasn't pleasant.

'Sorry I can't stay, work beckons.' Jack jumped up and headed out the door just in time to see Hazel ride up on a horse. She narrowed her eyes at Jack and dismounted.

'You.'

'Miss Brown.' Jack thought she looked quite

marvellous in her riding breeches and hacking jacket.

'What are you doing here?'

'I live here,' Jack said. 'What are you...' he didn't get any further as Mrs Sweetwater's prattle came back to him.

'You're the granddaughter?'

'Yes.'

'Mrs Sweetwater is your grandmother.'

'Yes obviously.' Hazel tied her horse under the shade of a sycamore tree.

'Mrs Sweetwater is your mother's mother.'

'Mr Renfrew, I think I know who I'm related to.'

There was a moments silence.

He should have just ended there. A laugh or two, a shared misunderstanding and that would be that. He should have kept his mouth shut.

'So you're the one who was left at the altar?'

Hazel narrowed her eyes at Jack. She pursed her lips which turned into a sneer.

'Is my grandmother at home?' Hazel pushed past Jack and strode into the house without a backward glance. If she had a whip she might have been the one to crack it.

Jack looked at the horse. 'Well, you could have told me.'

As the day stretched interminably ahead, the only recourse was to go back to the site and watch the concrete cure. It wasn't a great idea, but it was all he had.

On the road he thought on Miss Brown. Hazel was just complicating matters. He didn't need complications in his life, he needed a clear head.

He needed talent, tact and tenacity to get the job done. Although it's not something one puts on one's curriculum vitae, he was quite good at his internal monologue pep talk, not so red hot on the three t's.

Riding up to Torheit he was cheered to see the electrical truck on site.

'Hey there,' Jack jumped off the Harley and came over to the Zennith Union Electrification Company truck. He looked over the truck.

'New?'

'Yep.'

'Nice.'

'Yep.' The electrification engineer was a man of few words.

'So,' Jack struck a pose that might look like he knew what he was doing. 'How's it going?'

'Who are you?'

'Sorry, Jack Renfrew. V & K Project Manager.' He held out his hand.

'How do. Newton Parchmore.'

'Well, Mr Parchmore, how is work progressing?'

'It's not.'

'Pardon?'

This here site,' Parchmore scratched the back of his neck. 'No electricals.' Parchmore waved his hand in the air as if to conjure something from nothing.

'No.'

'Needs to come from somewhere son.'

'How far do you think?' Jack asked.

'As the crow flies?'

'Yes.' Jack hopped from one foot to another.

'About five miles. So I think you have a problem

right there.'

'Do I?'

'Yup.' Parchmore shoved his hands in his pocket.

Jack bit his tongue lest he say something inappropriate, which knowing his track record was quite probable.

'Oh,' he managed to say.

'And,' Mr Parchmore pointed, 'see them footings?'

'Yes.' Jack thought they looked quite lovely.

'No good.'

'No?'

'No.' Mr Parchmore walked over to the footings which were curing nicely. He scratched the back of his neck, picked up a stick and pointed to a spot in the distance. 'See that?'

'Um. What?'

'That.' Parchmore waved his stick. 'That'll be the electrical connection.' Jack squinted into the distance. He could make out a pole.

'Oh, the pole.'

'Comes over here and then,' Parchmore looked at the footing, 'needs to go in there.'

'Pardon?' Jack swallowed.

'In this here footing.'

'You mean?'

'Yup. We got to dig it out.'

'But we only just put it in.'

'Should've asked first is my guess.' Parchmore tapped the concrete with his stick.

'Well, can't we put it on the north side. We haven't done the cement yet.'

'Nope.'

Jack wanted to ask why, but was afraid it would

come out sounding like a whine or a whinge.

'Well, what about overhead?'

'Nope. This here's a warehouse. Got to be underground.'

'Warehouse?'

'Yup.'

'Mr Parchmore I think you will find this is designated a dwelling. A home.'

Parchmore frowned. He strode to his truck and pulled out a wad of papers and a drawing.

'This?'

'Yes.' Jack looked at a schematic of Torheit. He could see the confusion. It didn't exactly look like a home. 'It's an iconic building Mr Parchmore.'

Parchmore looked at the County Planning code signed by Mr Quill. 'And what about this?' Jack looked at the planning code.

'Quill.'

'Yup.' Parchmore looked at the drawing. 'I'll be back tomorrow. I need a new code signed by this fella Quill.'

'Quill.' Jack winced.

'I get my code, you get your icon.'

Brinkmanship *the policy or practise of pushing a dangerous situation to the brink of disaster in order to achieve the most advantageous outcome;*

There is always a little toing and froing in the art of negotiation. There is also a great propensity to make your opponent squirm. Jack squared his shoulders and asked Miss Delany if he might have a word with Mr Quill, immediately.

Miss Delany went into the office and came out again quite quickly. She shook her head.

'He's busy.'

'How about later?'

Miss Delany shook her head. 'I think he will be busy until a duck learns to tap dance'.

'Oh.' Jack studied the door. What would Mr K do? He'd bluster and puff. He'd rant and rave. He'd get the job done. If Mr Brown wanted his icon, he would get his icon.

Jack picked up his papers and made for the door. He took a deep breath and burst into Quill's office to the protestations of Miss Delany.

'I'm busy Mr Renfrew.' Quill sneered at Jack.

'Mr Quill. I need...' Jack was cut off.

'I'm not particularly interested in what you need Mr Renfrew.

Jack was about to cross the Rubicon. He tossed up the option of a rant or a stiff apology. Neither had appeal. Mr K might be able to pull off a hissy fit, but Jack Renfrew wasn't up to the task. The apology stung his sensibilities like Friar's Balsam on gravel rash.

'Er, Mr Quill, Freelan...' Jack smiled and tried to look tragically sorry for his withering remark the other day. 'I know you are a man with a powerful position. I know you have a myriad of pressing things to attend to, but if I could just have a minute of your demanding day.'

'Oh.' Quill was enjoying himself. Steerforth County Planning office didn't often get the chance to show its muscle and might. Freelan straightened his backbone. 'Mr Renfrew. You come busting into my office and expect me to just drop everything to attend to your whims and wishes?'

The men looked at Freelan's cup of tea and toast on his desk, the paper's squared away and the decks clean. A sarcastic crack tried to squeeze past Jack's lips. They remained as tight as a Scotsman's purse. He took a bracing breath through his nostrils.

'Mr Quill,' Jack pressed on. 'There is a discrepancy regarding the electrics.' Then Jack had a lightbulb moment. 'You just might be able to save the day.' Flattery is a powerful weapon.

'Oh.' Freelan sat forward and leaned on his desk.

'Oh, yes. Absolutely. Save the day. Yes.'

Jack explained the stupidity of Mr Parchmore not realising he was electrifying a dwelling. The absolute superior intellect of Quill to understand the subtleties of the architecture of an icon, and the small clerical error to give the electrification code a warehouse designation. All that would be needed was a new code drawn up and Quill might just save the day. 'We need it by tomorrow.'

The clock on the wall ticked as Jack waited. Freelan looked at the paperwork, then at Jack.

'Tomorrow,' Jack added.

'Intellect?'

'Superior.' Jack said. 'I'll wire Mr Kartoffelkopf and let him know it was Freelan Quill who made an icon rise from the Huff Parson quarter acre.'

'Really?' Freelan dropped his guard. To be mentioned in dispatches.

'I wouldn't be surprised in years to come your

name will be forever...well you know.' Jack smiled.
    'My name.'
    'Yes.'
The thought of immortality hit the right note.
    'Tomorrow you say?'
    'Tomorrow Mr Quill.'

Mr Freelan Quill (of superior intellect) dictates to Miss Lillian Delany.

CHAPTER 15

BROWN'S BROWN BRICKS STOP. DELIVERY IMMEDIATELY STOP. HUX III

Jack looked at the telegram and whooped. Finally things were coming together. What Huxley had failed to put on the telegram was the price.

The Schnider Kiln works had been trying to offload the brown bricks for some time. The foreman had christened them s&^* bricks and the colour put most customers off their dinner. It was an ideal opportunity to value add. V & K were practically begging for brown. Mr Schnider could see an opportunity when it presented itself. The quantity was discussed, the delivery was arranged and the eye watering price mentioned in passing. No-one passed out—always a good sign, and the deal struck.

'Get that s&^* out of here,' was heard on the loading dock.

The sun was shining and as Jack rode the Harley Davidson up the track to the site he broke out in a smile. Mr Parchmore was there, the Clutz clan were working, and then Skeet drove the dray on site with lumber and plenty of it.

'Morning,' Jack hopped off his bike and strode over to the men.

'Morning.' Parchmore said.

'Ah, Mr Parchmore, I will have your papers by,' Jack looked at his watch. 'about five minutes. Mr Quill is coming to deliver them personally. He wanted to see the site.'

Parchmore looked at his watch. 'Five minutes.' He walked to his truck and sat in it, pulled out a pipe and after packing it, lighting it, he stared into the distance and puffed.

'Mr Clutz,' Jack inclined his head.

'Howdy.'

'All fine and dandy?' Jack asked. Winslow gave a guffaw and jabbed Woodruff in the ribs with his elbow.

'Well son,' Mr Clutz stopped mixing cement and looked at the truck. 'I'd like one of them.' Clutz pointed to the Zennith Union truck. His old nag gave a whinny and deposited some soil improvement as a passing comment.

'Yes, modern machines are marching on,' Jack looked at the truck. It could carry so much more than a horse and dray. Woodruff gave Winslow a jab with his elbow and they giggled.

'Well, I won't keep you from your work,' Jack looked at his watch and noted the time—and there, in the distance, coming up the track on a bicycle, was Freelan Quill. He waved as he huffed up the rise. Vern signalled to Skeet to cover the lumber.

'Might rain,' Vern said to Jack's inquiring look.

'Mr Quill.' Jack held his bike while Freelan took off his bicycle clips.

'I thought you'd have an automobile?'

'I,' Freelan caught his breath, 'I ...thought...I'd ....exercise...fresh....air.'

'Right.'

'Have...papers.'

Jack snatched the papers and trotted over to Parchmore.

'I think you'll find these are more to your liking Mr Parchmore.'

'We'll see.' Parchmore tapped his pipe out and put on his spectacles. He read at an excruciatingly slow pace. He chewed over every word, every syllable as his lips moved while he read.

'Um, I'll just be over there,' Jack left the man to digest the document and found Quill looking at the footings.

'Footings.'

'Yes.' Quill eyed the Clutz clan.

'Quill,' Mr Clutz inclined his head and spat

'Mr Clutz,' Freelan narrowed his eyes.

'As you know...' Jack pointed out the features to Quill. As apple boxes go there isn't much in the way of Quoins, a Dutch gable roof or plinth blocks.

'That's the lumber and the bricks are coming in a day or two.' Quill looked at the lumber hastily being covered by Skeet.'

'Er, Mr Quill,' Vern Clutz drew Freelan's gaze to the view. 'Lovely ain't it?'

'Yes,' Quill turned back to the lumber.

'Er Quill,' Vern tried again, 'I'll get that paperwork to your office first thing. You know, the Casella job.'

'Ah.' Quill took out a pencil and a small note book. He wrote the name.

'This 'ere will be an icon Mr Quill,' Vern said.

'I know.'

'Well, I won't keep ya. Busy man that you are.'

'Yes.' Quill squared his shoulders and puffed out his chest.

'Absolutely. Nothing would happen if Mr Quill hadn't put his name to it.' Jack could butter up with the best of them.

'Well, it was only a small part.'

'Vital, I'd wager,' Vern said.

'Absolutely vital,' Jack offered and looked at his watch.

'Yes, time to go.'

'Be seein' ya.' Vern Clutz went back to work, one eye firmly on the retreating back of Freelan Quill as he cycled back to Brownsville.

'Pa?'

'Nothin' to worry about son. Nothin' at all.'

Freelan Quill cycled back to town with a whistle on his lips and feeling quite chipper. He was going to be practically immortal, and for a resident of Brownsville, a place that only warranted a small dot on the map, it was something to crow about. He was on the road and nearly sideswiped off it, by a large automobile, the klaxon horn giving him a fright.

'Watch it,' the driver shouted as the automobile sped past.

'Watch it yourself,' Freelan waved his fist in the air. Being immortal, one could still get run over. Freeland noted the driver, the make of the automobile and stopped to write it down in his little book.

It would be later, Freelan would discover the reckless driver was in the service of the Mayor and the errand of vital importance.

'Where,' Mayor Webster Wynkoop said as he sat at his desk and Freelan stood to attention in the Mayoral office, 'does a man get lumber at such knockdown prices?'

'I don't know sir.' Quill's superior intellect had deserted him.

The Mayor raised his eyebrow—he only had one, which extended all the way across his brow. Freeland felt faint. It was a rare event to be called into Mayor Wynkoop's office. At first he thought it was a summons to discuss his immortality, but the black look that greeted him dispelled that myth.

'You don't know.' The caustic words echoed in the office.

'No sir.'

'I'll tell you where, shall I.'

Freelan frowned. He didn't know if it was a rhetorical question.

'I have a better idea. Why don't you ask Mr Vernon Clutz? Perhaps he would know? What do you think?'

Rhetorical or not Freelan's epiglottis gave a gulp in reply. Like a sharp hit on the head with a two b' four, Freelan saw it all.

Mayor Wynkoop had seen it all, or to be more precise he hadn't seen anything at all...and that was the point. His golf club-house was short a load of lumber, the contractor, a Mr Gilbert citing delivery delays, although the bank teller, a Delany, a man who was prone to gossip and a snitch had banked the ill-gotten gains of Mr Gilbert just that afternoon, the exact amount withdrawn in the morning by Mr Clutz. It was all too much of a co-incidence. Small town rumours fly quicker than the starlings at dusk.

Mayor Wynkoop slapped his chubby hand on his desk. 'I want my lumber Quill.'

'Yes sir.'

'Whatever Brown is doing on Huff Parson's quarter acre it can stop.'

'Yes sir.' Quill stood still and blinked.

'NOW.' That made Freelan jump.

'Yes sir.'

There were a few people who wouldn't be happy about the outcome of the interview. Immortality didn't have such a shine. Freelan Quill, Steerforth County Planning Officer wished he was dead.

Of course one piece of wood looks much like another, so when confronted with an accusation the burden of proof would be a little tricky.

Quill sat at his desk, his head in his hands and dictated a letter to Miss Delany. He was just getting to the part about the accusation of theft or profiteering when the Mayor threw open the planning office door and bellowed.

'Still here Quill.'

Miss Delany's mouth dropped open, Mr Quill's eyes popped and the Mayor slammed the door on the way out.

There was a moments silence as the two recipients of the outburst collected their wits.

'Mr Quill?'

'Miss Delany.' Freelan jumped up, grabbed his hat and flew out the door. He doubled back, grappled his coat from the hook and legged it.

As he cycled to the Huff Parson's quarter acre he wasn't whistling, he wasn't feeling chipper and he thought capital punishment a fitting reward for the Clutz clan. A sneer developed on his top lip as he peddled out of town.

With time to ruminate on the facts with his superior intellect, he had, by the time he'd arrived, convinced himself that Jack Renfrew, Mr Brown, the Clutz clan and Mr Gilbert were all agin 'im and were probably laughing....at him.

As he rode up the muddy track to the site, Jack waved and shouted a cheery 'hellooooooo'.

'Quill parked his bicycle, and without removing his trouser clips strode over to Mr Clutz and pointed.

'Where,' he jabbed his finger at the lumber, 'did you acquire that lumber Mr Clutz?' Skeet, Winslow and Woodruff skulked away to the cement mixing.

'Lumber?'

'Yes, Lumber.' Quill's face was flushed. He gritted his teeth and huffed.

'From Mr Gilbert.'

'AH HA!' Sherlock Holmes couldn't have said it better.

'Something I can help you with Mr Quill,' Jack sidled up to the pair.

'You,' Quill looked at Jack as if he'd sprung from the underworld to take Freelan's soul.

'Pardon?'

'This lumber,' Quill pointed manically at the timber, 'it's not yours.'

'Pardon?'

'Ah.' Mr Clutz spat and hopped up from his footing. 'What Mr Quill here is trying to say I think, and stop me if I'm wrong Mr Quill, but what he's sort of accusing you of is taking this 'ere lumber from the job up the way and usin' it for your job.'

'Me?' Jack looked around for a witness, someone to hear the accusation.

'Is that right Mr Quill?'

'Er,'

'An' I think, now stop me if I'm wrong Mr Quill, but I think this 'ere lumber is belonging to the Mayor. Mr Wynkoop. Is that right Mr Quill?' Vern spat and put his hands in his pockets.

Freelan nodded.

'The Mayor?' Jack echoed.

'That's right i'n' it Mr Quill.'

Freelan found his voice, 'yes.'

'An' I guess, but stop me if I'm wrong Mr Quill, but I guess he looking for it back. Is that right Mr Quill?'

'Yes.' Freelan looked from Vern to Jack and back again. Vernon Clutz had neatly shifted the blame and no-one was quite sure how.

Jack looked at the lumber on the dray. He looked at Vern who shrugged and lit a cigarette. He glanced at Quill.

'Look. How about we keep this load and the Mayor can have our load.' Jack looked at Vern, 'our load is ordered isn't it?'

'That's about right.' Vern said.

'I'm sure it's just a delivery mix up.' Jack said.

'Ah, that'd be alright Mr Renfrew, but I paid for it see.' Vern said.

And then it all got a little confusing. V & K would reimburse Mr Clutz, the lumber would go to the golf club, Mr Gilbert would pay Mr Clutz and by the time everyone thought they had it straight someone was making a bit on the side and someone else splitting the difference.

Jack watched Skeet drive the dray down the road and disappear around the bend.

'I guess our lumber will be along soon.'

'No doubt,' Vern said.

'Bound to be.' Winslow added.

'These things happen,' Jack said philosophically.

'They sure do.' Vern spat as they watched Quill cycle away.

Watching concrete cure is a bit like watching paint dry without the colour. As the footings were finished the Clutz clan and Jack stood back and looked at the work.

'Give it some time.'

'Yes.'

There really isn't much to else to say when it comes to concrete.

'Er, the bricks will be arriving shortly.'

'That right.' Vern lit a cigarette.

'Yes.'

Luckily Mr and Mrs Browns buggy came down

the track to break the awkward moment.

'Ah. Mr Brown,' Jack pointed.

'Looks that way.'

'Mr Brown,' Jack almost galloped to the buggy.

'Howdy.'

'Mrs Brown,' Jack smiled.

'Oh, hello.' Enid was helped down and stood looking at the worksite.

'This it then?'

'Yes.'

'Why it's Newton Parchmore.' Enid put her hands on her hips.

'Enid Sweetwater.'

'Mr Parchmore is doing the electrification Mrs Brown.'

'It's not dangerous is it?' Enid looked at all the wires.

'Nope.'

'I'm getting a washing machine.'

'Is that so.'

'Electrical lights.'

'Ya don't say,' Parchmore said.

'All the modern conveniences. A machine that can suck up the dirt right off the floor.'

'Never.'

Mr Parchmore knew all about the vacuum machine. Mrs Parchmore had been bending his ear about labour saving devices ever since the spring catalogues had come in the post.

'And hot water Newton.' Mrs Brown added, 'by the gallon.'

'Fancy.'

'Oh yes. We intend to have an easy time of it,' Bill came into the conversation which went on for about a half hour, which Mr Parchmore added to the invoice. Easy money if you'd asked Parchmore. He'd talk all day at an hourly rate—although being a man of few words his 'consultations' were more in the way of listening.

Jack walked the Browns over the site pointing out the concrete.

'Yes, we see that.' Bill stood on the boulder and looked at the site.

'Oh, don't worry. In a day or two the first course of bricks. We got the brown.' Jack was hoping for an accolade or two.

'Bricks.'

'Yes.'

'Wanted to talk to you about the bricks.'

There was an ominous tone in the word bricks. Bill sucked in his guts and blew out through his nose.

'Yes?'

'Well son. We had a telegram.'

'Yes?'

'Don't often get a telegram.'

'No we don't often get a telegram.' Enid fished the missive from her handbag and handed it over to Jack. He read.

BRICKS NEED DEPOSIT STOP.

It might have read 'eyewatering amount,' as he looked at the zeros on the number.

'Ah.'

'That's a big number son.'

'Yes.' Jack wondered if he pulled his hair out would he feel any better.

'They're brown.' What can you say when your

spending someone else's money as if it fell, like manna from heaven.

'Now I don't know much, but this here seems a bit steep if you ask my opinion.'

Vern Clutz slithered up and looked at the telegram. He sucked his teeth and then shook his head. 'If ya had just asked me. I know a fella.'

'You do?' Jack started to clutch at the straw Clutz offered, then brought himself up sharp. He winced and bit his tongue lest he say something he'd regret.

'A fella,' Bill took the straw and was about to run with it.

'Mr Brown, we've got your bricks. They are perfect for this build. They may look a little on the luxury end, but I assure you, they will be a defining feature.'

'A defining feature,' Vern said and spat.

'Yes Mr Clutz.' One can't put a price on an icon.'

'I've got a pretty good idea on the price son, a pretty good idea.' Bill put the telegram in Enid's handbag and walked back to his buggy.

⅓

'I'll be back later,' Mr Parchmore was packing up his truck. 'When the framing and the outer bricks are up, just let me know.'

'Yes. Certainly.' Jack took his card and noted he had a telephone. 'I'll ring.'

'Yup,' and Newton Parchmore did a three point turn and was gone.

'I'd sure like one of them,' Vern said watching the truck make the turn.

'Well, you could always just take it and call it a misunderstanding,' Jack sniped.

'I could, but who'd believe me son, who'd believe me?' Vern whistled up his sons and they drove the nag down the muddy track.

'Will you be here tomorrow?' Jack yelled.

'Just try an' keep me away son,' Vern laughed as they rounded the bend.

CHAPTER 16

With Jack's week rapidly coming to an end he inspected his pillow for hairs, looked in the mirror for a bald patch and braced himself for the avalanche of things to do.

The most pressing question was what would Mr Clutz be doing in Jack's absence? The answer might make a man take to drink.

'Something the matter Mr Renfrew?'

'Nothing, Mrs Sweetwater,' Jack dipped his soldier toast in his soft boiled egg.

'You'll be off the day after I presume.'

'Yes.' Jack took a sip of tea.

'Coming back?'

'I hope so Mrs Sweetwater.'

'Well, I know we will be glad to have you.'

'We?'

'Did I say we? Well, I know the Browns, *all* the Browns, will be glad to see you when you come again. I'll keep your room open shall I?'

'Please.' Jack finished breakfast and took his dishes to the sink thinking, *all* the Browns might encompass half of Brownsville and about a quarter of Steerforth County.

'Oh, you leave that alone Mr Renfrew. Get along now.'

'If you're sure?'

'Git.' Mrs Sweetwater shooed him out of the kitchen.

'Er...'

'Yes?'

'Mrs Sweetwater. I wonder if you know of the Clutz family at all?'

'Vernon Clutz. Of course.' Jack needed some leverage. He'd heard all about Mr Quill, the man, the moods, the mother and now if only he could get something on Clutz. It might be a trump card.

'It's just that he's...' How do you describe a scoundrel, a rogue, but a builder who didn't need to subcontract and promised a tender under budget. A tricky one at the best of times.

'Oh, don't you worry about the Clutz clan. They might be slippery as an eel in jelly, but Bill and Vernon go way back.'

'Do they?'

'Oh yes. Those two were the terrors of Steerforth County. You wouldn't know it to look at them now.' Mrs Sweetwater patted an imaginary stomach. 'Just you remind Vernon where his hot dinners came from all those years ago.'

'Hot dinners?'

'That's right. Mrs Dolly Brown, Bill's old mother, treated Vernon like a son. Practically dragged him up.'

'Really.'

'Vernon knows which side his bread is buttered.' Mrs Sweetwater collected the remaining dishes and started to wash up. The way Jack saw it, Vernon Clutz wanted the stick of butter and the loaf of bread, perhaps to sell it back to V & K at double the price.

The news of Vernon's loyalty to Bill the man rather than Bill, the bank balance, gave Jack some comfort. He dressed for the motorbike and after filling up with gasoline rode to the site with his list running through his mind.

Zennith electrification.

Bricks.

Jones plumbing and drainage

Lumber

Windows

His first stop was the telegraph office. There was a message which might have made a lesser man turn grey on the spot.

K COMING TOMORROW STOP WILL NEED LUNCH STOP HUX III

Jack slumped on a bench and groaned.

'Everything alright?'

'Huh?'

'I said, everything alright.'

Jack nodded.

'I have another for you.' The woman behind the counter held out the other telegram.

LUNCH AT AUNTS STOP ABSOLUTE DARLING STOP DON'T WORRY STOP OYSTERS A LA CARTE STOP HUX III

Jack sat back and breathed a sigh of relief. Good ol' Huxley. What a friend. When you've had bad news and then good news it puts a spring in your step and the sun begins to shine, in a metaphorical sense anyway. Jack looked out the window of the office and saw ominous dark clouds building on the horizon.

'I think it's going to rain,' the woman said following his gaze.

'I hope not.'

Two other customers looked out of the window and there ensued a lengthy discussion on the weather. If ever you are in a rural farming community there are one or two subjects that should judiciously be avoided—the weather and the price of feed. You might have plans for the day, but get a farmer started on the weather and you might be, by the end of the conversation, closer to your funeral arrangements than your thoughts of pork chops and a quart of milk when you set off that morning.

Jack, being the polite chap that he was, listened to the men discuss the likelihood of rain, the rain they had in '78, the rain that was expected in '88 and the rain that didn't arrive in '97. The conversation was peppered with names he didn't know, places he hadn't been and dates before he was born.

'I remember...' the gentleman began when Jack made a show of looking at the time, and said in a loud voice,

'Oh my, I must get on.' He bolted for the door shoving his telegrams in his pocket and after strapping on his goggles, slipping his hands into his gloves, high-tailed it to Torheit, the rain cloud chasing him down the road.

There was a great deal of activity on the site. None of it to do with actually building Torheit.

Good news. The bricks from Schnider Kiln Works had arrived.

Bad news. The truck from Schnider Kiln Works was bogged in the muddy track.

Good news. The Clutz clan were unloading the bricks.

Bad news. They were doing it one at a time.

No-one had thought the thing through. Jack could see right away that the bricks being stacked on the ground would be in the way.

'Er, Mr Clutz.'

'Mr Renfrew.' Vern stopped working, which stopped the sons working.

'I wouldn't presume to...'

'Well don't.'

'Right.' Jack pursed his lips and looked at the weather. 'I think it's going to rain.'

He got a humpf in reply.

The Schnider men sat on the boulder and watched the men work.

'Hello.' Jack scooted over and held out his hand.

'How do.' They nodded and tapped out their pipes on the boulder.

'I think it might rain.'

'Could be.' The Schnider twins looked at the clouds.

'Will you be able to get out of the mud?'

'Likely will,' the first man said.

'Yup.' Number two added. 'Just as soon as,' he pointed the stem of his pipe at the Clutz clan. They all watched the men work. There is something quite cathartic watching other men work. It is mesmerising and almost poetic. The toil of man. The labours of muscle to move mountains, to forge valleys, to move bricks from one place to another... for Vern had woken up to the fact that he had put the bricks in an inconvenient spot.

Jack pursed his lips before a tempting 'I told you so,' slipped out.

It took the old nag all he had to pull the truck clear of the mud.

'Still want a truck Mr Clutz?' Jack held the horse and patted its head.

'My oath I do.' Vern looked at the truck belch smoke as it made the turn and trundled down the track.

'They will be back with another load in a week.'

'Ol' Bill picked these, did he?'

'Yes.' They studied the bricks that looked nothing like dark chocolate, mud or tanned rich deep brown leather.

'No accounting for taste eh?'

'None whatsoever.'

No sooner had the Schnider truck departed when Bill drove up in his buggy followed by Hazel on her horse.

Jack immediately struck a pose of a man who looks like he knows what he's doing. Skeet, Winslow and Woodruff carried on counting bricks while stifling giggles.

'Oh hello,' Jack waved and came up to the buggy.

'Miss Brown.'

'Mr Renfrew.' Hazel hopped down and tied her horse to the buggy.

'The bricks Mr Brown.'

'I see that son.'

'They're brown,' Jack said.

'So they are.' Bill said as father and daughter stared at the pile of bricks.

'Another load next week.' Jack kicked a sod of mud from his shoe.

Hazel gazed at the ground. It was churned, rutted, sodden and resembled a battlefield. 'They are footings,' Jack pointed. Hazel bit her bottom lip and smiled. 'No doors Mr Renfrew?'

'Not yet.' Jack said then realized the joke. 'Ah.'

'Well I just came down to take a look. Mother said the electrification was under way.'

'So it is.' Jack pointed to a cable sticking up from the ground and a roll of wire.

'Will ya look at that,' Vern pointed to a cart coming up the track. 'It's Parsnip Jones.'

They all watched the cart make its way to the site and a small pointy black man pull his horse up with a 'whoa.'

'Parsnip.'

'Clutz, boys' The clan doffed their hats and Vern spat. 'Parsnip.' Bill inclined his head and touched his hat.

'Brown.' Jones tipped his hat.

'Mr Jones,' Hazel said.

'Miss Brown,' Jones replied.

Everyone was being introduced except Renfrew.

'Excuse me,' Jack said a little too loud. Everyone stopped and stared.

'Plumber. Parsnip Jones.' Mr Jones held out a

knobbly hand.

'Jack Renfrew, Project Manager for V & K Architects.' Jack took the hand. He looked at Mr Jones. There was no doubt why he was called Parsnip. His nose resembled the root vegetable and no mistake. The formalities over Jones pulled a scrap of paper from his overalls pocket and handed it to Jack.

'Is me list. I'll be needin' someit to get started.'

The list was extensive. Pipes, joiners, taps, copper do-dads, thing-a-me-bobs and do-hickies. The figure at the bottom of the list was a bit more than a water butt and a bucket.

Vern slithered up and took a look. 'Ya got the copper yet Parsnip?'

'Nope.'

'Leave it to me.'

Jack hated those words.

'I know a fella.'

He hated those words even more.

Bill looked at the list. He developed a tic in his eye.

'I'll be a fixin' the pipes once the frame is in.'

'I see.'

'Layin' the ground water, the drainage and such right now.'

'Right.'

Jones looked over the site. He crinkled his nose and closed his eyes, Jack hoped, envisaging the maze of pipes needed for a modern home.

'Mrs Brown's wanting a washing machine contraption.' Bill brought out his little black book and the crowd melted away. Even the strongest of wills can only stand to hear about bath plugs, taps and soap holders more than a dozen times.

'An' I'm fixing on having my gentleman's bathroom with hot water.

'Ahuh.' Jones licked a stub of pencil and made a note.

'And I've ordered some taps.'

Ahuh.' It was written on the back of an envelope.

'And I figure on a wash stand with one of those shaving hot towel things.'

'Ahuh.' Jones nodded.

Bill bent Parsnip's ear for a good twenty minutes as Jack toured the site with Hazel.

'Grandmother said you're the best guest she'd had by a long shot.'

'Really.'

'She said you're a darling in the kitchen. Helping and such.'

'Did she?'

'Hmmm.' Hazel stood on the boulder and looked at the view.

'Nice isn't it.'

'Oh yes. I always liked this view.' Hazel took it all in.

Jack took all of Hazel in as he gazed in her direction.

'Um. Mr Kartoffelkopf is coming tomorrow. To have a look.'

'Oh.'

'Yes, and then he's having lunch at Huxley's aunt's place.

'His aunts.' Hazel smiled. 'I like Roman.'

'Me too.' Jack said. He would have liked a three toed sloth in a dinner jacket had Miss Brown indicated they were a favourite.

'I was wondering if you and your parents would care to join us for lunch?' It was a bold assumption that Jack might be invited to lunch with his superior. Usually apprentices were delegated to a polony sandwich while the partners of V & K picked the wine and made their way through the various silverware on offer. (always start at the outside fork and work your way in).

'Are you sure?'

'Oh yes. The more the merrier.' Jack didn't give a thought to the catering, the seating, the invitations or the social standing of the guests.

'Thank you Jack.' Hazel touch his sleeve and smiled, 'we'd be delighted.'

The two watched Parsnip edge away from Bill and bring out a tape measure.

'I'll leave you to it Jones.'

'Much obliged Mr Brown.' Parsnip almost ran to his cart and hid amongst the various pipes and fittings.

'He's going to dig a hole,' Bill said adding a bit of pomp as if he was the one who found a pencil so they might write the declaration of Independence.

Vern and sons watched the plumber with interest. Parsnip was a one man whirlwind. He dug a hole. He made a trench. He laid a pipe, looked at the plans and made a connection or two and by the late afternoon there was a network of clay pipes throughout the site looking very orderly, professional and logical.

'Alright there Jones?'

'Yes thanks.' Parsnip stopped for a sandwich.

'Was just wondering about a spigot?' Vern dug

Skeet in the ribs and smirked. Seeing a man so organised, dedicated and methodical put the Clutz clan on edge. And when you are on edge there is nothing like a bit of ribbing to even the score.

Parsnip looked at the plans. There was to be a collection tank at the top of the site, gravity feed then a pump.

'I can give you your spigot Clutz.'

'Oh.'

'Once the electric pump is installed, should be no problem. No problem at all.'

'Oh.'

Winslow, Woodruff and Skeet bent their backs to the work at hand. Vern put his plug of tobacco in the other cheek and spat.

'So that's about it.' Jack handed the list over to Vern.

Handing a list to a builder is like giving a bald man a comb. Vern looked at the list, frowned at Jack and shoved the paper in his overall pocket.

'I will be back, only I don't know when.'

'Don't you worry about a thing Mr Renfrew. I've got everything under control.'

Those words didn't instil confidence in Jack. He looked at the slow pace of the Clutz clan, the dilatory way they did everything including breathe, and their disregard for the 'right' way.

'This here icon of yours will be well on the way when you come back.' It sounded like a jibe. It felt like a jibe. Jack tried to look on the pragmatic side of things.

'Well, Mr Kartoffelkopf will be here tomorrow.

If you have any queries, I'm sure he can clarify things.'

'I'm sure he can.' Vern sucked his teeth and spat.

Mr K arrived at Torheit in Huxley's Pierce Arrow 66.

He stood up and cocked his Tyrolean hat on one side, threw his cape over his shoulder and declared,

'Ah—fresh air.'

'Ah—sky.'

'Ah—lunch.'

There was no need to labour the point when one was invited to a hyphenated residence—with a butler.

CHAPTER 17

Mrs Waldo Harrington-Croaker, widow, was a lively woman of independent means. Mr Waldo Harrington-Croaker croaked quite early in the relationship leaving Lydia Mavis H-Croaker with a sizable fortune. Lydia lived life to the full and then some. She was a Huxley in her maiden years, so having been born with a silver spoon in her mouth, she knew all about silver service, trips to the Continent, who was related to whom and what wine to serve with potted pheasant and duchess potatoes.

Money, old or new could get you things you'd only dreamt about.

Mr K cleaned his glasses and positioned them to take in the view. He stood back and admired the bank balance one needed to indulge oneself in architecture. The Harrington-Croaker pile of bricks had every architectural influence that one could dream up.

Aunt Lydia Mavis Harrington-Croaker in her hay day.

Grecian urns, Roman colonnades, Georgian fronts, Corinthian topped columns, Tudor stained glass and one wouldn't be surprised to see a Welsh coracle on the lake or a Swiss chalet as a stable.

Jack winced at the columns. Roman waved the umpteen dozen urns away, 'don't look too hard Renfrew. Croaker had more money than sense.' *Or taste,* Jack thought.

Bill looked at the house, 'I bet they've got hot water.' Enid nodded, 'and a washing machine.'

'Now, now everyone.' Huxley stood on the steps to the front door and gathered the guests together.

'Don't wander and don't get lost. Follow me.'

Jack grabbed Huxley's arm as they went through the enormous front door, 'are you sure it's alright?'

'Aunt Lydia will be delighted.' Huxley ushered the Browns into the receiving hall and the butler took their coats and hats.

'This is Wearing.'

'How do.' Bill shook the butler's hand.

'Sir.' Wearing bowed graciously.

'Oh,' Enid curtseyed, her new hat jiggled and bobbled as she ogled the finery.

'This way.' Huxley led the luncheon party through the library...

'Oooo, will ya look at that.'

...past the bust of Caesar

'Oh my word.'

...into the conservatory

'Oh, Lordy lord, have a plant Edie.'

...and onto the lawn terrace.

'Carry me out with the tongs!'

'Father,' Hazel jabbed Bill in the ribs as they stood and admired the manicured lawns, the artificial lake, the fountain (a genuine replica from France) and the folly (another genuine replica, from Scotland. The Harrington-Croakers get around.)

'Aunt Lydia.'

'Roman.' There was a flurry of kisses, then introductions.

Mr Kartoffelkopf blossomed. He loved the grandeur, the opulence, the splendour of the place. This, he felt, was where he belonged. These people were his people.

'Madam,' Mr K bowed low, gave his hand-waving a work out and came up for air with a smile.

'Pleasure.' Mrs H-Croaker said.

The Browns were struck dumb by the performance of Mr K.

'Mr and Mrs Brown. My Aunt. Mrs Harrington-Croaker.'

'How do Mrs Croaker.' Bill managed to squeak out. Enid smiled and curtseyed.

'Oh, call me Lydia.'

'Oh, I couldn't Mrs Croaker. It wouldn't be right.'

'Nonsense. And you are...?'

'Enid and Bill.' Enid said. 'I'm Enid,' she added with a giggle of nerves.

'Well, Enid, sit down and Wearing will get you a drink. I know I could do with a stiff one.'

'Oh.' Enid sat.

'Miss Hazel Brown and Mr Jack Renfrew.'

'Ah. Roman has told me all about you,' Lydia pointed to Jack. 'And,' she took Hazel's hand, 'you're the young lady with the driving school. Am I correct?'

'Yes. That's right.' Hazel smiled.

'Well, this will be fun. Sit down everyone.'

One can quickly get accustomed to the trappings of wealth. In no time at all, the gang were knocking back mint julips made with gin like they were born to the role.

'They're quite nice aren't they?' Enid took another from Wearing.

'So, Mr Renfrew, Jack. I hear you are the man of the hour.' Jack shot a look at Mr K. He didn't want to usurp his superior's position. There was only room for one genius at the table.

'Well...I'm just the project manager,' he

deflected the accolade, 'Mr Kartoffelkopf is the architect for the building.'

'It's an icon Mrs Croaker,' Bill said with a small slur. Mint julips have a habit of sneaking up on an empty stomach.

'I'm sure it is Bill.'

'Mr Kartoffelkopf's design will be quite the defining moment in architecture,' Huxley said.

'Really.' Lydia raised her eye brow.

'Ever since man has wanted to build,' Mr K began with raised finger in the air, 'after the expense, after the durability, comes the aesthetic enjoyment.' Mr K ended with a wave of his mint julip. Jack crossed his fingers and hoped that was true, because Torheit still looked like an apple box, no matter what spin you might put on it.

Wearing hovered, 'Lunch Ma'am.'

'Shall we?'

Hazel almost dripped off Huxley's arm as they walked into the conservatory for lunch.

'Your aunt is such a sweet, isn't she.'

'We think so.' Roman propelled Hazel to a chair with his hand in the small of her back. Jack noted the hand, the gaiety, the conviviality of the gesture.

'I'll sit here, shall I?' Jack scooted to the empty chair on Hazel's left. 'Mrs Brown would you like to sit here,' he leaned across and held the chair on Hazel's right for her mother.

Mrs H-Croaker and her nephew exchanged a look with Wearing. The butler coughed and politely pointed out that at luncheon the guest should be seated alternating the sexes.

'I think if Mrs Brown would sit here,' Wearing pulled out a seat for Enid, it would be quite satisfactory for conversation.

'Oh.' The social faux pas glanced off Jack who was on his third mint julip.

'If only Lucria were here,' Huxley sighed, 'love of my life.'

'Oh.' Jack perked up, just a little.

An elegant luncheon in a conservatory with table service, fine wine and desserts to die for, can loosen ones inhibitions, make one feel gay, happy and full of pep. The gang were expansive, ebullient and effusive.

Mr K talked of the three Fs as if he'd invented them, holding his finger in the air. Bill explained the ins and outs of a bath plug. Hazel regaled the company on the idiosyncratic foibles of her many students, quite forgetting the teacher/student confidentiality clause. Jack gave a demonstration of the spitting techniques of Mr Clutz and Enid espoused on the benefits of a machine that can suck the dirt right from the floor.

'Machines do everything but suck eggs,' she said, defining the modern industrial age in one fell swoop.

Mrs Harrington-Croaker hadn't had such a lively bunch for lunch since the Derby in '97.

'I think we'll take tea on the terrace Wearing.' It sounded innocuous enough, but to the hoi-polloi it was a moment to savour and wonder if...one day... they too might utter... 'tea on the terrace Wearing' the ultimate moment in being filthy rich.

Fond farewells took about twenty minutes as everyone said their party piece, everyone assured Mrs H-Croaker that they had the time of their lives, and everyone issued invitations to their respective abodes. Then another twenty minutes was needed to discuss who was going with whom and who was being dropped off, picked up and left behind.

Logistics were decided. Mrs H-Croaker would summon her driver Stuart, who would take Mr and Mrs Brown home. Huxley, Mr K and Hazel would scoot back to the city in the Arrow.

'Now you be sure and pop on over when our house is done.' Enid nodded and held onto her hat as she sat next to Bill in the Cadillac Model 30.

'Just tell Stuart where to go won't you.' Mrs H-Croaker waved.

Jack turned his cap around and put on his goggles, 'I'll be back in the office tomorrow sir.' He buttoned his jacket and smiled at Hazel. She caught the smile and returned it.

'The office?' Mr K, who was feeling magnanimous with around five mint julips and two glasses of a smooth red frowned and cocked his head to one side.

'Work sir. At the office.' Jack noted Hazel's smile and blushed.

'No, no. YOU will continue.'

'Sir?'

'You are with your people,' Mr K turned from the front passenger seat and waved his hand at the Browns in the back seat of the Cadillac. He then gave a gracious smile to Mrs H-Croaker like an orphan hoping to be adopted or at the very least invited to become one of the 'set'.

Having to stay behind, wiped the smile off Jack's face. He was hoping for more convivial lunches, more walks in the park, drives to the hills, picnics and intimate dinners with Hazel. The prospect of more spitting, more mud, more of the same wasn't appealing in the least. Jack gave a pleading look to Huxley, but there wasn't much Roman could do. When Mr K made up his mind, that was that.

Jack would be, at the end of the day, depositing his feet under Mrs Sweetwater's kitchen table once again.

The rendering of Torheit lay on the Brown's kitchen table. The lads in the dungeon had done a marvellous job with the modification of brown bricks, the drawing looked quite real.

'I thought I'd bring it straight over. It came in the post this morning.' Jack picked the salt shaker and the sugar bowl and held down the corners of the drawing.

Bill put on his glasses and gave it a good going over.

'I think it's quite modern,' Enid said as she set out cups and saucers for a pot of tea.

'Modern,' Bill said. 'Er, what are all these?'

Jack came in for a better look. 'Delphiniums, I should think.'

'And this?'

'Another urn sir.' Bill went urn hunting. Putney had gone to town in regard to urns. Swindon had supplied the floral arrangements and Steinbeck the odd plinth or two.

How many urns a mid-west farmer needs would be a source of wonder for years to come.

'Well, I think it looks quite iconic.'

'Oh yes Mrs Brown. It's iconic.' They all looked at the apple crate, the bricks drawn expertly and neatly coloured within the lines in a fairly descriptive brown pencil.

'You'll want to know Hazel is coming home for the week. Wants to see her new niece, Daphne.' Mrs Brown set out some biscuits and as if on cue, little Daphne set up a howl.

'That'll be Daphne,' Enid smiled and poured a cup of tea for Beth, and trotted off to the nursery.

'A week?'

'That's right,' Bill dunked his biscuit.

It didn't take long before the site of Torheit was awash with lumber, bricks, pipes, wires and quite a bit of soil improver courtesy of the various horses. Jack helped stack bricks, move timber beams, shovel sand, hold pipes and unravel wire. As the build progressed there was a frizz in the air. To see something grow, become more than two dimensional enlivened the workers. It was inspiring, thrilling and satisfying.

Parsnip Jones stood back and scratched his nose. He squatted down and looked at the bathtub.

'Sure is a mighty fine bathtub.'

'From Mr McCreedy's Porcelain Emporium,' Bill said as he gazed with affection at his bathtub still in its packing crate.

'Ya don't say.' Parsnip took in the fancy legs, the rolled lip, the large plug hole and the enamel in arctic white. They stood with the plans in hand and took in the measure of the gentleman's bathroom.

'Yep, sure is a fine bathtub.' There was something quite gratifying to know your plumber approved of your purchase.

Anything plumbing related had a special place in Parsnip's heart. He was just one of those fellows that loved his job—a rare breed. Mention a U bend and Parsnip would put you on his Christmas card list. Extol the virtue of nickel plated hardware and you'd likely be in his will. Bill and Parsnip looked at the tub.

'She'll need to go in before the door.' Jones extended his tape measure and reacquainted himself with dimensions. 'Yep, she'll need to go up there through that gap and that ought-a do it.'

Bill had had a hard time justifying the brown bricks. It seemed everyone had an opinion on the bricks; from the postmistress to the knitting circle, Mrs Delany going so far as to say they reminded her of something, but she was too polite to say what.

'Wait until you see the taps,' Bill strutted around his, yet to be walled bathroom, envisaging the day his dream might come true.

Vernon Clutz took a nail from his mouth and hammered it into the last floor plank. He stood up and stretched his back.

'All done son.' He looked at Jack.

'I'm not going to ask where you acquired the nails Mr Clutz.'

'That's the idea son.' Vern winked at Winslow who was sweeping sawdust.

'The windows should be here any day now Mr Clutz.'

'Right you are son.'

ᚼ

'They're not right son.' Vern looked at the glass on the cart and then spat.

'Not right?'

'Too small, look.' Vern brought out his tape measure and put his finger on the problem. 'Won't fit.'

They stood and looked at the windows, then at the delivery driver who was feeding his horse.

'Don't look at me, I only deliver 'em.'

'Well, they'll need to go back.' Jack gave the invoice back to the driver.

'Now, hold ya horses a minute son.' Vern shifted the plug of tobacco and looked at the glass. Reckon I know a fella might want 'em.'

'Really?' Jack said a little too eagerly. And then there was a confusing moment where Brown would get a refund, Mr Clutz would get a discount, the difference would be deducted from the quote, the glass manufacturer would sell his windows to Clutz, who'd deduct something from someone and someone else would get 4' ¾" by 2' ¼" clear, green tint glass windows.

It would be later, someone would pay double for windows that just happen to fit the cloak room of a Golf Club-house in the vicinity. A serendipitous co-incidence.

195

When something like an icon is being built there is bound to be a bit of interest. A Golf club is nice, but an icon, well that's a different ball game.

Mayor Webster Wynkoop 'Web' to his friends, liked to keep his finger on the pulse of Steerforth County. He wanted to know who was doing what—and to whom, but inevitably, as a member of Government (a small member) he was quite possibly the last to know. Mrs Delaney had more of a handle on the ins and outs of Brownsville, the word on the street and the various peccadilloes of the 'Steerforth set'.

Once the news of an icon filtered to the Mayoral office, Wynkoop ground his teeth and wanted to know why he wasn't informed. Freelan Quill tried to ingratiate himself, but it wasn't working.

'I didn't know sir.' Freelan tried to sound convincing. When you're dealing with being immortal in regard to an icon there is only so much room at the top of the pedestal.

'Are you or are you not the Planning Officer?'

'Yes sir.'

'And you didn't know.'

'No sir.' Freelan crossed his fingers behind his back.

The Mayor strutted around his office. 'I thought it was a house,' Webster said.

That was his first mistake.

'I thought...' That was his second mistake. Politicians, even small ones, aren't paid to think. Quill received a dressing down. His ears were smarting from the vitriol. The vitriol was passed down to Miss Delany who told her mother —and by the time the news that the Mayor didn't know his Arthur from his Martha, Mrs Sweetwater was regaling Jack with the facts over pork chops and apple sauce at the end of the day.

'Webster was always a sulky little boy,' Mrs Sweetwater said. 'He was called whiney Wynkoop, or sometimes nincompoop. Children have a capacity to cut to the quick sometimes.'

'You seem, to know everyone as a child Mrs Sweetwater,' Jack helped himself to more potatoes.

'I was the only school teacher round these parts.

'Oh.'

'You have trouble with any of these whippersnappers just let me know.'

'I'll do that Mrs Sweetwater, I surely will.'

A golf course and club-house may be just what the Captains of industry desire in the county, but Webster Wynkoop knew the publicity of an icon was worth a bit more. He may be slow on the uptake, but once he got there—there was no stopping the man. If V & K had a baby he might have kissed it for the camera. As it was, he designed a photographic opportunity for the local paper.

Jack got wind of the impending visit via the knitting circle and sent a telegram to head office.

LOCAL PRESS INTERESTED IN TORHEIT STOP HOW TO PROCEED STOP

It didn't take long for a reply. It didn't actually say 'you have total control' but reading between the lines, Jack felt he had the gist of the thing.

PROCEED WITH PRESS STOP STANDARD

PROCEDURE STOP USE DISCRETION STOP

When someone says to use your discretion, it can imply you have the wherewithal to use your brain to its full capacity. Jack didn't exactly know what standard procedure was in this regard, but how hard could it be to say a few words to the press. He had never heard of the word 'angle'. There is always an angle when the press is involved.

The rain the previous evening had turned the site into a bit of a mud puddle. What with carts, wagons, horses, trucks and people, it was beginning to look like a stock yard after a spring sale.

The photographer and a reporter arrived by automobile and surveyed the site. The Mayor came up the track in his automobile and looked at this shiny shoes, then at the mud.

'I have boots if you'd like sir.' Jack offered a pair of boots.

'Just put a plank down will you.' Webster waited for Skeet to bring a plank and begin to lay a track across the mud to higher ground.

'Rain.' Jack said and smiled.

The photographer followed the Mayor and then the Browns arrived and Mr Quill.

'Quill?'

'Mayor Wynkoop.'

Freelan wasn't about to be usurped. As immortality stood, he wanted to be first in the queue.

'If I could just have a snap?' The photographer called to the crowd.

Getting a plumber, a builder and his three sons, a Planning officer, an electrical engineer, one Mayor, a project manager and Mr and Mrs Brown in the one spot at the one time was no mean feat. The photographer, Louis Powell did his best.

'Now if you'd all just hold,' he shouted as they stood on the new flooring amongst the frames. 'I'll just snap a photograph.'

The word snap might denote a quick click. And in normal circumstances that would be all it would take, but Louis was a bit of a fuddy-duddy. He liked to go all artistic. He liked to get that perfect shot. He had the people frozen with smiles that looked more like autopsy pictures, than a happy bunch of people building an icon.

'And one more.'

There was an audible groan as they stood still.

'And that's it,' Louis said.

Bill rubbed his face to get his cheeks working again.

'And what do you think Mr Brown, of your icon?' The reporter, Alec Griggs asked.

'Well...' Bill Brown wasn't quite comfortable being put on the spot. He liked to chew the thing over, give it some thought, mull over the thing with his full consideration. If it was the weather, or the price of feed, or bathroom fittings, then he was on sure ground, but put him on the spot and he floundered.

'Well, I...' He sucked in some fresh air.

'Yes?' Alec waited with pencil and paper.

'I'm sort of hoping...'

'Yes?'

'Well, it's...' Bill scratched the back of his neck.

'Modern,' Enid came to the rescue.

'Yep, it's modern.' Bill said.

'All the modern conveniences.'

'Yes, that's right. All the modern conveniences,' Bill echoed his wife. Alec wrote it down.

'And do you think it might be a talking point?'

'Oh yes.' Bill nodded and tried to escape. 'He's the one,' Bill pointed to Jack and made a hasty retreat.

'Mr Renfrew?'

'Yes.' Jack looked over at the young reporter.

'The project manager?'

'Yes.'

'And how are things progressing?'

'Very well. Everything is on schedule and on budget.'

The Clutz clan could be heard chortling in the background.

'How does it feel to be building an icon in Steerforth County?'

'Oh, it's all in a day's work,' Jack said trying to remain nonchalant and businesslike.

'Really?' Alec wrote it down.

'Well, when I say that, what I mean is...' and Jack's enthusiasm got the better of him. He talked about the build, the cost, the vision of V & K, the artistic temper of Mr K, the acumen of Mr V and the adventurous foresight of Mr Brown. He didn't miss the bit where Mr Brown was cajoled, flattered and enticed into such a modern build. He couldn't leave out the bit where Torheit was the baby of Mr K and he'd been trying for ages to get someone 'willing' to undertake the project, having had several setbacks already.

Alec wrote it all down...and then some.

'So it's a bit of a white elephant then?' Alec asked.

'Pardon?'

'Well, Mr Kartoffelkopf wanted someone, anyone to build it.'

'It's an icon Mr Griggs.' Jack looked at the Clutz clan sitting in the fire place on the boulder smoking.

'That'd be icon with a capital I?'

'Absolutely.'

'And you are?' Alec asked the chap who was hovering and trying to insert himself into every interview.

'Freelan Quill. That's Quill with two ls. I'm the planning officer for Steerforth County.'

'So this,' Alec swept his arm wide to take in the building site, 'is all up to you?'

'Yes.'

'And the Golf club?'

'What?' Freelan began to dislike the press. 'Nothing gets built that doesn't pass my desk.'

'Is that so?'

'Absolutely.'

Alec collared the Mayor.

'What do you think Mayor Wynkoop?'

'Me? I think its selfish gratification of riotous invention.' They turned and looked over the building. 'Brown,' Webster said and rolled his eyes. 'Can you think of a more boring colour?'

'Not off the top of my head,' Alec said.

'Reminds me of something.' The Mayor smirked.

'Can I quote you?'

'Heaven's no.' Webster looked at the reporter.

'Looks like an icon to me.'

'Can I quote you?'

'Absolutely.'

'Looks like an apple crate to me,' Alec said.

The Mayor took another look at the thing. He knew it looked familiar. Now he could see it, he couldn't un-see it.

'Apple crate,' he laughed all the way back to his automobile, and was still chortling half way back to town. At least his Golf Clubhouse didn't look like an apple crate. His Golf Club-house looked more like selfish gratification of riotous invention. It had about a dozen more urns than Torheit for a start.

IS STEERFORTH COUNTY READY FOR AN ICON?

The headline gave a flavour of the article to follow. Alec Griggs had gathered all the threads and come up with a white elephant that might be a blot on the Huff quarter acre, when all the hoo-ha was stripped away. A brown edifice that no-one wanted. A modern contrivance born of an imposing ego. V & K might do well in the city, but Steerforth county was definitely not the big city, and country folk knew a dodge when they saw it. The Mayor didn't come out very well, looking as if he'd been duped and his Golf Club-house usurped in the 'what's new in Steerforth County' stakes.

The whole thing stank like a swindle without actually saying the word. The slant was towards honest farmer Brown and his faith in modernity, innovation and trust. Honest farmer Brown was the perfect innocent abroad. He was done like a dog's dinner.

And to top it off, the paper had purloined the drawings and reproduced Bill Brown's house with a Jim Dandy Apple label stuck on it.

Mayor Webster Wynkoop read the piece and called the Editor of the Brownsville Daily Echo, who just happened to be a Captain of industry with a short handicap. A small column was discussed throwing light onto Wynkoop distancing himself from the Brown building. His interest so far removed it was about as hard to see as the 18th hole from the clubhouse, (a particularly bad design flaw that had the golfers hiking half the course for a cold drink).

Freelan threw the paper in the waste basket.

'They didn't even mention me,' he bleated to Miss Delany.

'I should count your blessings Mr Quill.'

'Eh?'

'Well, you don't want people to think you are so dumb to be conned by V & K? Do you?'

'No.'

'And you don't want your name associated with an apple crate? Do you?'

'No.'

'So the less said the better.'

'Yes. But they said I'd be immortal. My name forever associated with Torheit.' Freelan's voice went up an octave as he whined.

Miss Delany shook her head.

'No?'

'No sir'

'Absolutely.' Freelan looked at the paper. He might have been duped once, but once was enough. As the planning officer of Steerforth county he was about to wreak his revenge. He was about to make Jack Renfrew's life a living hell.

CHAPTER 19

Having put his faith in the press, Jack didn't bother to purchase a paper. He blithely carried on as people in the street pointed him out. He waved back. Brownsville residents stood and stared as he rode down the road. He gave a cheery 'helllooooooo,' and carried on thinking country folk were so friendly once you got to know them. Mrs Sweetwater was unaware of the hoo-har as she purchased the paper later on her morning shopping round. But once she had read the news, it was all hands on deck. Family is family and no-one puts one over a Sweetwater or Brown. Clara Sweetwater ordered a horse and trap

Who would have imagined the circulation numbers of a small town paper would be so large. Jack stopped in the queue of vehicles, horse and buggies, pony and traps, bicycles, rubber necks, gawkers, and busy bodies lining the muddy track to Torheit.

'Pardon me. Excuse me.' Jack made his way to the front of the line and parked his bike.

'What's all this?'

Vern scratched his head and sucked on his tobacco plug.

'Well...it's all on account of the paper see.'

'The paper.' Skeet said.

Woodruff and Winslow looked at a husband and wife as they walked over the newly laid floor planks.

'Excuse me,' Jack narrowed his eyes and struck a pose.

'Oh, that's him.' The woman said, pointing with a gloved hand.

'This is a work site Madam.'

'Oh. He says it's a work site Harold.'

'Please leave.' Jack put his hands on his hips.

'Oh. He wants us to leave Harold.' The woman echoed. For a fleeting moment Jack wondered what the conversation would be like if the woman and Skeet might be married. It didn't bear thinking about.

'NOW!'

That got the pair moving. They retreated to a tuft of grass and lollygagged.

'What's going on?' Jack watched a man start picking up rocks.

'Eh, leave those alone.'

'Just the one, a souvenir.' The man pocketed a rock.

'Mr Clutz?'

'Mr Renfrew,' Vern pointed to a fellow striding through the throng of people. 'I think that's Mr Quill.'

And so it was.

Freelan shoved his way to the front and found his mark. He pointed to Jack and ground his teeth.

'You.'

'Me?' Jack smiled. 'Mr Quill. Another visit. So soon?'

'I was informed you are arranging site-seeing tours. That would constitute a business. You are not authorised to conduct a business from this residential block. There are licences you know.'

'What?' Jack frowned and shook his head as Vern & Sons melted into the back ground.

'Licences.' Quill produced a sheaf of papers and waved them in Jack's direction.

'But I'm not conducting tours. I'm not doing anything at all.'

'HA.' Quill said to make the point.

Parsnip Jones nodded in agreement. He'd yet to see Jack do much except run about trying to organise everyone. Parsnip was one of those fellows who don't take kindly to people telling him how to do his job.

'Are you the fellow we pay? Only I don't have much time and I wanted to see what all the fuss was about,' a stout man proffered a coin to Quill.

'No.'

'The fuss?' Jack asked.

The moment was interrupted by Bill, various Browns and Mrs Sweetwater.

'Oh, hello.' Jack spied Hazel in the mix and trotted over to help her off the trap.

Hazel looked at the hoi-polloi. 'Quite a turn out isn't it.'

'Yes, but for the life of me I can't understand

why.' Jack shrugged his shoulders.

'Perhaps this will help.' Mrs Sweetwater gave the paper to Jack and they all stood back while he read every word, some phrases twice. He folded the paper and closed his eyes.

'Mr Renfrew?' Freelan Quill poked his adversary in the back.

'Huh?'

Freeland waved his papers of cease and desist in Jack's face. 'You will cease and desist until a full accounting of the violation has been attended to by the relevant authorities.

'The relevant authorities?' Bill asked. 'What's going on?'

'Freelan Quill.' Mrs Sweetwater put on her school mistress voice which made the assembly sit up and take notice.

'Yes Mrs Sweetwater?'

'Ever since second grade you have been a model student. Courteous, kind, quiet and studious. Now you are a bully Freelan. Just a plain hog-wallowin' bully.'

'But I just...' Freeland shuffled his feet. He felt about six years old.

'You will give this young man time to get his affairs in order.'

'I will?'

'You will stop this nonsense and let Bill Brown get on with building his...' and here Mrs Sweetwater looked at the course of brown bricks and the framework, 'his *modern contrivance.*'

'I will?'

'Yes, Freelan you will.' Mrs Sweetwater had spoken.

The assembled crowd broke into applause and a cheer went up. Freeland went from immortal to mediocrity in less time than it takes to ask the barman for a double shot of the elixir of life.

The crowd had come out to see a *modern contrivance* and witnessed a dressing down of local government for the same price. If there is one thing to unite the plebeians it is someone sticking it in the eye of local government. Freelan began to slink away, muttering oaths, curses and undying retribution.

'Mr Quill,' Jack handed back Quill's papers, 'Listen, this will blow over. I'm sure it's just a misunderstanding. I should imagine once Torheit is built, the fan fair, the hoo-har will be consigned to history. Our names will go down in a book somewhere and that will be that.'

Freeland looked at Jack as if he had sprouted two heads.

'Immortal. Pfft.' He picked up his bicycle and cycled out of history, or so he thought.

'A hog-wallowin' bully?' Enid said and jabbed her mother in the ribs.

'Well...' Clara Sweetwater winked.

The crowd ogled at the Browns as they ogled at the crowd. Not much happens in Brownsville, so when one gets the opportunity to ogle, one often takes it.

'What's all this hog hollarin' son?'

'Well...' and Jack explained the shenanigans, the chicanery and the flim-flam. 'And that's about the size of it, Mr Brown.'

And then, all eyes were on the Clutz clan, who were working diligently at their labours.

'Er, Mr Clutz, if I could have a word,' Jack squared his shoulders for the confrontation.

'Well folks,' Bill looked at the lollygaggers, 'I guess you folks all want to know about this here house we're buildin'.'

Getting it straight from the horse's mouth was more than the gawkers could hope, for the price of admission.

It was a proud moment when Bill led the crowd to his newly purchased bath still in its packing crate and extolled the virtues of hot water, soap holders, and the ins and outs of bath plugs. Meanwhile, Enid was telling the ladies,' sucks the dirt right off the floor!' There were exclamations, coo's and ahh's as modern conveniences at affordable prices were discussed in great detail. By the time the crowd had thinned and departed no-one thought the Browns had been duped. No-one thought the house a white elephant. Everyone thought they might quite like a bit of modern living at affordable prices. Word of mouth beats an advert in the Brownsville Daily Echo every time.

The Quarterly Architectural Gazette, a dour publication with about as much dazzling style, flamboyance and flair as... well let's say a brown brick, somehow (Mr K knew someone on the board) picked up the story of Torheit and ran with it. The chap on the board also had interests in a daily paper in the city...and... it didn't take long before the story was reproduced, twisted, massaged and pummelled into something the city slickers could understand while eating their cornflakes. Someone found the story in the Brownsville Daily Echo and put two and two together and came up with about half a page with illustrations. The story grew legs, as they say in the industry and it wasn't long before every paperboy knew the initials V & K. What no-one bothered to do was get it from the horse's mouth, that is until Alec Grigg received a telephone call from a city daily hoping for an 'angle' as they like to describe a more lurid perspective of a tired story.

And that was how Torheit turned from a white elephant into a shining example of good ol' American know-how and modern living for everyone—just like farmer Brown.

The front page said it all.

YOU TOO CAN HAVE ALL THE CONVENIENCES

Ad men can see an opportunity while sitting on a bar stool at fifty paces. This opportunity hit them in the face like a wet fish. It was too good to be true.

The office of V & K buzzed with the news. Mac fielded telephone calls from all quarters.

Washing soap? 'Just a sample, to see if Mrs Brown likes it.'

Electric iron? 'Of course if Mrs Brown likes it, well she might give us a word or two.'

Does Mr Brown shave? 'Our bristles have the added benefit of massage.'

And all of it absolutely free!

Mac sat back with her cup of tea and took the phone off the hook.

'Busy?' Huxley said as he came out of Mr Vs office with an empty coffee cup.

'You've no idea.' Mac sipped her tea and pointed to her pile of notes.

'What does,' Huxley hoiked his head at Mr Ks office door, 'think of it all?'

'Oh you know. Genius cannot be bought,' Mac laughed, 'except when it's all free.'

'There is always a catch I've found,' Huxley said.

Jack looked at the man touting a box of soap powder.

'There is always a catch,' he said.

'Not here. Mother's soap flakes are happy to give Mrs Brown their superior product absolutely free.'

'Oh my word,' Enid Brown looked at the young salesman.

'And we,' a man who looked like he could sell sand to an Arab began, 'we are willing to go one better.' The salesman tipped his hat back and put his thumbs in his waistcoat pockets. His audience hung off his every word, 'We at Shindock washing machines will add a mangle. Absolutely free.'

'Oh.' Enid frowned.

'Free Mrs Brown.' The man stood back to let the offer sink in.

'Mother?' Hazel looked at her mother's

expression. To Enid all this sounded a bit like giving a man a free shovel and telling him to dig a hole. It's all work no matter how you say it.

'That's all very nice of you I'm sure.' Enid bit her finger nail.

'Well, Mrs Brown, we'll leave you to think on it.' The Browns watched the men walk to their trap and disappear down the track.

No sooner had they gone than another trap came up the hill.

'Another one,' Hazel said and sat down on the newly made steps.

'Hellooooo,' a thin man cooed and doffed his hat. 'The Browns I assume.'

Bill nodded.

'Mick McCreedy,' he held out his hand as he stepped down from the trap.

'McCreedy?'

'That's right. From...' He didn't need to finish as Bill put two and two together,

'McCreedy's Porcelain Products.'

'At your service Mr Brown.' Mick gave a smile.

Parsnip Jones stopped his pipe work and narrowed his eyes at the representative of McCreedy's Porcelain Products. Jones didn't say much, but when he did he had quite a few words to say about Mr McCreedy's business acumen.

His nick-name amongst the plumbing fraternity of Mc Greedy just about summed it up.

'So, Mr Brown,' and Mick launched into a lengthy spiel on just what McCreedy's could do for Mr Brown, how much it might cost Mr Brown and how the grand vision of those pioneers all those years ago could now be realized by Mr Brown... with the help of his vision, his drive and his wallet. It kept the Clutz clan, Parsnip Jones, Parchmore, Jack and the Browns enthralled, even the horse stopped eating.

'And, Mr Brown, McCreedy's will add a soap holder, plus a bath plug at no extra cost.'

'A bath plug.' Bill was a happy man.

A noise rather like a pulled bath plug escaped Parsnip's lips. 'There is always a catch,' he said under his breath.

And as Torheit rose from Huff Parson's quarter acre the offers piled up. Electric waffle maker, General Electric irons, electric toasters, electric light switches and then...the doozy...a Hutton hot water system at a discount of 10% from the Standard Sanitary Manufacturing Company. Parsnip looked at the letter outlining the offer. He studied the schematic diagram noting the nut sizes, the pipe flaring, the intricate thing-a-me-jigs. He whistled in admiration at the specifications.

'What do you think Parsnip?'

'Well Bill, I think it's a mighty fine piece of modern engineering.' That was all Bill needed to hear. He puffed out his chest. He looked at the drawing of the Hutton hot water system.

'Yessiree, mighty fine.' Parsnip said. No-one would be surprised to see Bill's name on Parsnip's Christmas card list. As plumbing apparatus go, the Hutton was the pinnacle of excellence with brass things, two way switch bits, and a safety valve made with the finest bronze do-dads.

It seemed everyone with a modern convenience at affordable prices wanted a piece of the action.

Mayor Wynkoop went from not touching Torheit with a barge pole to practically bending over backwards to be associated with an icon. Politicians, even small ones, are known for their acrobatic back flips, so much so, they could apply for a job at the circus. Politics is a circus at the best of times, so if the shoe fits...

Mr Quill, although harbouring murderous thoughts, was actively trying to wheedle his way back to immortality.

Such is the power of a trend, a craze, a fashion.

It was a fine sunny morning when Jack stood back, squinted, shielded his eyes and said,

'Um, I'm just wondering.'

'Yes?' Vernon Clutz stood and admired his handy-work. The walls were up, the windows were in, the roof was on.

'Well,' Jack looked at the plans in his hands. Skeet shot a look at his brothers and they suddenly found their fingernails, their boots, the horizon quite riveting to the eye.

'It seems to me...'

'Yes.' Vern said trying to downplay the moment. He knew what was coming. The Clutz clan had known since the first stick of dynamite how a silly little mistake might blow up in their faces. Now the fuse was lit.

'Mr Clutz,' Jack looked at the plans and turned them this way and that. He held them up to the light and it dawned on him as a first ray of sunshine to break the horizon.

'It's back to front.'

'Beg Pardon?' Vern spat and used his boot to cover the wet patch. He would need more than a clod of dirt to cover this mistake.

'It is built back to front.' Jack felt the blood rush from his head. He found a few bricks and sat down.

'Now don't go getting all funny about it son.' Vern patted Jack on the back.

'Funny?'

'It'll do just fine.'

'Fine?' Jack was beginning to sound like Skeet.

'Looks better this way, don't it?'

A noise like the sucking of mud down a drain hole escaped from Jack. He dropped the plans and held his head in his hands.

'Mr Clutz...'

'Hmmm?' Vern picked up the plans and handed them to Jack.

'Take them away.' Jack could see his whole career gone. Just like that. Poof.

'Now, listen.' Vern pulled Jack to his feet. 'We got to look at it from a different angle.'

'And which angle is that Mr Clutz,' Jack snapped.

'Well it seems to me that an apple crate looks the same any which way. Now this here house don't seem to have a back or a front if ya ask me.'

'No-one asked you Mr Clutz.'

'An' well, I reckon with the door over yonder, well Bill and his wife will have no trouble getting' inside when they be old an' doddery.'

'Doddery.' Jack said. He looked at the building. As it was built up to the hill, Clutz was quite correct.

The front, now back door, was level with the land and a convenient path. Bill and Enid wouldn't need to climb the front steps to their door.

'You think...'

'I do.' Vern patted Jack on the back.

'And they...?'

'Won't even know.' Vern said.

Bill, Enid and Hazel stood in front of Torheit and watched the delivery dray trundle up the track. It had the Hutton hot water system on board and this, in Bill estimation, was a red letter day and not to be missed.

'Careful there,' Bill hovered as the two burly lads hauled the crate to the ground. Parsnip looked over the crate and nodded in approval. The men began to gather all the paraphernalia that goes with a Hutton hot water system.

'Where do you want it Mister?'

Bill looked to his plumber for expert advice.

'Inside.'

The men looked for a door. 'Where's the door?'

'Huh?'

'The door Mister.'

'Er...' Bill looked at his house. He scratched his head. He frowned.

'Er, Jack,' he called, 'can I have a word?'

Jack was busy with Hazel and probably wouldn't hear a freight train if it came up and bit him on the ankle as he ingratiated himself to Miss Brown.

'Hello there.'

'Hello Jack.' Hazel looked at the house.

'Nice isn't it.'

'Yes.' Hazel smiled and adjusted her hat in the breeze.

'It's looking quite modern don't you think?'

'Yes.' Hazel said.

'You know Mr William Morris said, have nothing in your house that you do not know to be useful.'

'Did he?'

It wasn't intended to sound like a lecture, but Jack just couldn't help himself.

'or believe to be beautiful.' Jack ended.

'Like a door?' Hazel had a way of saying things that sounded like sarcasm. She just couldn't help herself.

'Ah.' Jack said and tried to smile.

'Hmm.' Hazel pursed her lips to stop herself from giggling.

'Jack,' Bill shouted.

'Hmm?' Jack came back to the present with a jolt.

'Where's the front door?'

Hazel couldn't contain it any longer. She burst out laughing. 'Have nothing in the house that you do not know to be useful Mr Renfrew?'

'Well Mr Brown, it's there,' Jack pointed to the rear of Torheit.

'Right you are.' The delivery men began to haul their cargo up the rise.

'But...' Bill began, 'I thought...'

'Yes?'

'It's just that I thought...'

'What?'

Now came Jack's coup de grace. He took a breath

and said, 'Torheit is a balance between architectural and constructional means. The building retains its freshness and leaps over the transition period that usually precedes the crystallization in a building of a new architectonic concept.

'Oh.' Bill shut up. No-one likes to be seen to be ignorant of their architectonic concepts. Especially when they are paying for them. Jack stood back and watched the plumbing apparatus make its way to the back door with Parsnip in attendance.

'I'll just go and take a look,' Bill followed his hot water tank. Enid tagged along.

Jack and Hazel gazed at Torheit.

'Modern.'

'Yes.'

'You've done something marvellous Jack.'

'Have I?'

'Oh yes. Quite marvellous.' Hazel gave Jack a peck on the cheek.

Sometimes, having a degree in architecture can be a bonus when, against all the odds you remember that one quote that might get you out of trouble and is bound to impress. It doesn't happen often, but when it does...oh boy!

Of course getting a Hutton hot water system into a gentleman's bathroom when physics dictated twos into one won't go is another matter. Jack stood back and let Parsnip take care of the details, he was too busy walking on air.

CHAPTER 20

'Where's the front door?' Huxley whispered to Jack as they stood back from Torheit.

'Don't ask.' Jack said through the side of his mouth.

'A bit like that is it?'

'Definitely.'

'Mornin' Mr Quill.'

'Clutz.' Freelan said with a modicum of derision.

'Nice day for it.'

'For what?' Quill narrowed his eyes.

'The shindig. The press Mr Quill.' Freelan whipped his head around and realised he had walked into history. Here was his chance to shine a light on his vital position in the scheme of things. It was just a pity his ego wasn't nearly as big as Mr V or Mr Ks self-worth. Minuscule by comparison.

The press arrived and piled out of their

automobiles, their jaded views on life, people and the world in general hung over them like a darkening thunder cloud. Most city press men had seen it all—and written about it—but Torheit had them stumped. As one, they stood back to take it all in. There wasn't much to take in as one apple crate looks much like the next.

'Any good bars around these parts?' one of the more jaded reporters asked Vernon Clutz.

'Not much to look at is it?' a fellow with a bowler hat said.

'Reminds me of something,' a hack with a homburg said, pointing to the brown bricks.

'Mr Toffelpop.' A reporter licked his pencil for a quote.

'It's Kartoffelkopf, ja.'

'Right.' The reporter rolled his eyes wondering why he always got stuck with the Kartoffelkopfs, the Swicynskis, the Lollobriganinos and the Vichnobscopts. Where was someone with a name that he could spell.

Freelan Quill hovered in the background as Mr K drew breath and the reporter waited. We've heard it before, but Mr K found a new audience. He held his finger high. He postulated on art, genius, the making of man yadda, yadda, yadda. Then Mr V had a few words to say as Freelan skulked around the periphery.

'We make something, no?'

Mr K polished his glasses then snapped them back in place. 'There is no price for art ja?' If Bill Brown had been listening, he could have put a price on it down to the last nut and washer. The reporter closed his note book and blew out a deep breath. Even seasoned reporters have a limit for aggrandisement.

'Thank you.' He beat a retreat.

'Oh, are you from the Morning Daily?' Jack asked the weather-beaten man with a weather-beaten hat and coat.

'Yes, Noel Braithwaite.'

'This is Mr Brown, Mr Braithwaite,' Jack said while Freelan lurked just out of earshot.

'Pleased to meet you sir. Very pleased indeed.' The reporter pumped Bill's hand like he was inflating a bicycle tyre.

'So...' Noel began. The next twenty minutes was reserved for Bill, 'That's just plain ol' Brown. B.R.O.W.N?'

'That's right.' Bill took his twenty minutes. Mr Braithwaite heard all about a house that would have all the bells and whistles, all the whizz bang contraptions and probably all of Bill's money.

'It's an icon Mr Braithwaite.'

'So I heard,' Noel said. They looked at the house. 'Icon.'

Freelan loitered as the men gazed at Torheit.

'Yep.' Bill studied his house. There was no doubt it was iconic, different, unusual, modern, and that favourite, a new architectonic concept.

'And tell me Mr Brown, do you like it?' Well, someone was bound to ask the question sooner or later. Mr Braithwaite had seen it all, and he knew how to get to the nub of the issue.

'Well...' Bill pursed his lips. 'It...' he scratched the back of his head and sucked air through his teeth. He shuffled his feet and frowned and bit his lip. He shoved his hands in his pockets and took a good long look at Torheit and the crowd quietened down, the birds stopped chirping, the mud stopped sucking on people's shoes and everyone waited. Noel poised his pencil over his pad.

'You know,' Bill began, 'I...'

The only sound was Mr Clutz shifting his baccy plug from one cheek to the other... 'I think I do.'

And from the depths of the house came a clamour and a strangulated howl, then a couple of thumps a few loud bangs and a wheeze.

Parsnip poked his head out of the bathroom window,

'We have hot water.'

A collective cheer erupted on the mound.

'A Miracle ja?'

'A Miracle no?'

As miracles go Bill paid about $450 for his. 'Worth every dime.' It was a quote Mr Braithwaite considered a bit of a miracle himself.

The gaggle of reporters, builders, plumbers, owners and architects milled and shuffled around the site dodging the horse soil improver, the mud and the detritus that builders often collect in vast amounts.

'Very brown isn't it,' said the bowler hat.

'Very oblong looking wouldn't you say,' said the homburg.

'Modern, no,' Mr V said to a skinny fellow from the sports pages who was subbing for the modern living editor while she was off sick.

'Ya don't say,' he kicked a clump of dirt.

Mr K strutted and struck a pose for his picture.

Louis Powell took his time with the light, the pose, the composition. Although on the staff of the Brownsville Echo, Louis was adept as spreading his expertise about the place. He'd cornered the market pretty early on when the city papers descended on Torheit. Now he had exclusive rights.

'Just a second more,' he said to Mr K.

'Like this ja?' Mr K obliged.

Hazel looked at the spectacle with her arms folded over her chest and a frown on her brow.

'I think the word you are looking for Miss Brown is narcissist,' Huxley said as he sidled up to her. Hazel smiled. She wasn't as quick to judge, not out loud anyway.

'You're looking well. Love the hat by the way.'

'Thank you Mr Huxley.' Hazel touched her new hat with a large pheasant feather whipping about in the wind.

'So...what do you think?'

'I think I need to get back to the city. All this...' Hazel waved her arm in the direction of Torheit, 'is too much hoo-har for me.'

'Quite.'

'And you Mr Huxley?'

'I'm the chauffeur,' he inclined his head towards Mr V and Mr K.

'Right. And then lunch?'

'Absolutely. You wouldn't care to join us?'

'Oh, I don't think so.' Hazel looked over to Jack who was talking to a reporter.'

'Ah. Prior engagement?'

'Yes.' Hazel nodded at the trap. There was a picnic basket in the back.

'Splendid.'

'I think so.' Hazel smiled.

Mayor Webster Wynkoop pulled up in an automobile and jumped out, 'am I too late?' He squelched across the mud to Braithwaite and shook his hand. The Mayor had no shame and came out for publicity much like a fair weather man on a Swiss thermometer clock.

'Marvellous, simply marvellous. Your work is outstanding.'

'Thanks.' Braithwaite said.

'An architectural masterpiece.'

'Isn't it just.' Braithwaite nodded.

'You must be very proud.'

'Me?'

'Yes.' The Mayor felt his ingratiating wasn't hitting the mark. Usually his gushing, his fawning was top notch.

'To design something like this, its...its...genius.' Wynkoop gestured at Torheit.

'I guess so.' Braithwaite caught on. This fellow thought he was Kartoffelkopf.

'You are to be congratulated.'

'If you say so.'

'Mr Kartoffelkopf, can you stand next to that urn?' Louis yelled from his high vantage point. The Mayor looked to Braithwaite, then to Mr K who was trying to mimic something out of the Roman Empire.

'Mr Kartoffelkopf?' Webster pointed to the Caesar on the rise.

'Looks like it.' Braithwaite put his pencil behind

his ear. Mayor Wynkoop strode off in the direction of Caesar.

'Be seein' ya.' Braithwaite smirked and watched the Mayor dodge mud puddles on his quest to be ingratiatingly irritating.

'Er,' Freelan tapped Mr Braithwaite on the sleeve.

'Hmmm?'

'Freelan Quill.' The name didn't immediately register with Braithwaite.

'And?'

'Steerforth County Planning Officer.'

'Oh, right.' Braithwaite had seen enough small egos in his tenure at the newspaper to recognise the species when he encountered it in the wild.

'How do you spell that?'

'Q.U.I.L.L'

'Right.' Braithwaite wrote it down to mollify the beast.

'I was the one to set the wheels in motion. Nothing gets built in Steerforth County without my say so.'

'Is that right?'

'Absolutely.' Quill said and might have given himself a pat on the back if he could reach around that far.

'County Planning Officer?'

'Yes.' Quill watched Braithwaite write it down.

'So, you would be the one who gave the tick of approval to the Mayor's Golf Club?'

'Pardon?'

'The Golf Club. The one down the road built on prime farming land and the farmer was only paid less than six cents an acre instead of about seventy cents.'

'Well...I...'

'Hmm?' Braithwaite waited. To say the moment wasn't quite what Quill expected was the understatement of the year. Freelan hummed and hawed.

'Look, here is my card,' Braithwaite said. 'When you want to talk, just let me know.'

'Yes. I'll do that.' Quill swallowed an uncomfortable truth and watched the reporter stroll away. He added reporters and the Mayor to people he didn't like.

Jack was feeling quite chipper as Mr V and Mr K strolled about the site, smiling, gesticulating and basking in the attention. He was feeling so chipper he let his guard down and so when the punch to the guts came it was quite out of the blue.

'WHAT?' Mr K's voice carried over the site.

'I was just asking,' Noel Braithwaite said, 'where the front door might be?'

Mr Kartoffelkopf wheeled around and his eye caught Jack like a punch to the solar plexus. Everyone turned to look at Jack, then they looked at Torheit, then back at Jack. Quill actually let out a small scoff.

'Ah.' Jack wondered if he could trot out his quote, but thought better of it. A wise move as Mr K's wrath began to boil.

'Yes, Mr Karttoffpop, where is the front door?' the homburg asked.

'Kartoffelkopf,' Mr K snapped and looked at Jack. He wasn't the only one as every eye was on the, soon to be unemployed, project manager.

'Well, it's like this...' Jack began. He gave a small giggle, a habit when nerves get the better of him and looked over to the Clutz clan. Vern smiled and winked.

'JA!' Mr K's look left Jack in no doubt that whatever he was about to say, it needed to be brilliant, genius level at the very least.

'Torheit is built on the three Fs principal.' Jack swallowed and held his finger aloft. Imitation is the highest form of flattery although it is a fine line between imitation and parody.

'Form follows function.'

The assembled crowd was silent, digesting the words that sounded like they should be inscribed in stone.

Mr K narrowed his eyes at Jack. He cocked his head and frowned.

'And don't forget my architectonic concepts,' Bill said.

That did it. Mr K looked at Torheit.

'Ja! Architectonic concepts.' He was a lover of big words and this one was stunning, breath-takingly magnificent.

'We make man to our own designs no!' Mr V added.

'Ja!!' Mr K deserved two exclamation marks. He took off his glasses and gave them the once over.

It all sounded wonderful hogs wallop to the newspaper men. The papers could have a field day with the parody, the satire, mockery and caricature of over inflated, self-congratulatory, high-falutin', poppy cock.

But as they say, any publicity is good publicity. The name on everyone's lips would be Torheit. The name synonymous with architects would be V & K.

'By the way,' Noel Braithwaite asked Jack as he was walking to the automobile, 'where is the front door?'

Jack waved in the general direction of the hill. He felt the less said the better.

'You know Jack,' Huxley began, 'Herodotus asked Croesus or some fellow in history, who is the luckiest person in the world, and you know what his answer was?'

'No.' Jack let out a humongous sigh.

'The man who is not dead yet. Or something like that.' Huxley patted Jack on the back. 'Still breathing?'

'Yes.'

'Keep doing it Jack. That's the trick.'

When the circus had departed, and Jack had retreated to the main room of the house to collect his wits, Hazel sought him out.

'Feeling alright?'

'Huh?'

'Are you feeling alright Jack, you look pale.'

'Oh, I'm alright.' Jack felt he'd had his intestines pulled out, wrapped around a rim joist and then shoved back in with a timber truss.

'Huxley said you had a bit of bother.'

'Did he?'

'Hmm. Said you'd be alright though.'

'Did he?'

'Yes. He said you'd probably get a bonus when this is finished.'

'Did he?'

'That's what he said. He also told me to say that you still have your hair.'

Jack touched his hair. He felt great sympathy for Edgar, and knew exactly why he was in California.

'Would you like some lunch?' Hazel put her basket down and sat on the boulder which was the centrepiece of the hearth. 'Eat.'

There was no doubt Hazel Brown was from good stock. When the female line of the Sweetwater clan command you to eat, you eat.

CHAPTER 21

Bill and Enid walked around the empty rooms and tried to envisage how to make a house a home. Someone once said, decorating is easy, just pay double and tell everyone its fashionable. Bill knew just how that fellow felt.

The Browns stopped in front of their enormous fire place and looked at the boulder.

'Nice,' Enid said, thinking of the family gathered around the fire, marshmallows and hot chocolate. Bill poked his head up the chimney, 'Coo,' he said marvelling at the dimensions.

They walked through the rooms, stopping at the gentleman's bathroom to admire the plumbing.

'Oh Bill,' Enid took her husband's arm.

Bill had no words to describe his utter delight at his fixtures and fittings. 'Coo,' he said as he regarded the 'absolutely free' soap holder and bath plug from McCreedys, but it was the Hutton hot water system that dominated the room. 'Ten percent off,' Bill said and fiddled with the levers and knobs.

The new-fangled flushing toilet had their admiration. Enid flushed and they watched the water swish around the bowl and disappear.

'Here, let me have a go,' Bill pulled the chain and then watched the water swish around the bowl and disappear. You can see there isn't much to it, as it does the same thing time after time. Enid did it again and the Browns congratulated themselves on having such a wonderful contraption.

'Beats going outside, doesn't it?'

'Sure does.' Bill pulled the chain one more time.

From there they went to the gentleman's dressing room and then the master bedroom.

'Oh my word,' Enid said. The room looked enormous. 'I could walk a mile just to get a hair pin.'

'Room to move,' Bill strode around the perimeter marvelling at the elbow room. Mr Vuoto was designing a bed of ample proportions to fit a room of such a generous size. In fact Mr V was generously designing all the furniture for Torheit. The office of V & K were full of generosity. So full in fact that their generous proportions added quite a generous dollar amount to the build, the size of the furniture and their fee.

'Room to move,' Bill reiterated. Now he wouldn't need to share his wardrobe space with his wife, his dressing table with hair pins and lipstick, his sock drawer with his wife's stockings.

'Bill, look at this,' Enid had found her way to the kitchen.

'Big.' Bill looked at the empty space.

'Yes,' as women are apt to do Enid was first to spot a problem. 'but where is the kitchen sink?'

'The what?'

'The sink Bill. Where is my kitchen sink?'

'Well, it's got to be around here somewhere.'

They looked. Nothing popped out.

'Are you sure this is the kitchen?'

'There's the pantry. There are the electricals. And it has a chimney for the new stove.'

'Right.' Bill said, 'wait here,' and he went looking for Mr Clutz.

'So Vernon, this is the kitchen so where is the sink?'

'Ah.' Vern took his hat off and scratched his head.

'Ya want a sink?'

'I do.' Enid said. 'I ordered a sink. I'm sure I saw it somewhere.'

'Always wantin' someit don't they?' Vern said to Bill. The remark didn't go down well. Bill loved his wife, and if she wanted a kitchen sink, well, she should, by golly, have one.

'Vernon, we paid for a kitchen sink. We want a kitchen sink.'

'Alright, alright, hold ya horses Bill. I can get ya a sink. I know a fella.'

'Bill,' Enid pursed her lips.

'Leave it to me Mrs Brown.' Those words coming from anyone else might have instilled a level of trust and expectation. Coming from Vernon Clutz, well, sometimes it's best not to get your hopes up.

'A kitchen sink,' Jack said as his shoulders slumped.

'That's right son.'

'Right.'

Looking at the problem with Parsnip Jones, Jack realised there was more to the job than just putting a hole in the floor for a drain and then a sink on top. The floor joists would need reinforcing, the drainage reworking, the 90 degree thing-a-me-bob would need adjusting with the doo-dad, then the hot water routed and the floor re aligned.

''bout a week,' Parsnip said.

'Right.'

'Two weeks,' Vern Clutz said of the floor joists and the realignment. 'Might cost a bit more, but these things can't be helped.'

'And did you by any chance see Mrs Browns sink delivered?'

'Not that I recall.' Vern spat.

'Right.'

On the off chance, Jack hopped on his Harley and went for a ride in the direction of the Golf Club. He came back with a sink strapped to his bike and the builder's curses ringing in his ears.

'Delivery men these days,' Vern said, 'practically illiterate. Sheesh.'

'Illiterate,' Skeet said.

A woman has an eye for colour when it comes to paint. Enid had a bit of an idea on what she wanted, but decided she should consult her daughters and daughters-in-laws. Seven women descended on Torheit with colour swatches, bits of material and scraps of wool. Bill beat a retreat to the kitchen to watch Parsnip at work, a much more satisfying endeavour than listening to women.

The women convened in the master bedroom and amid sandwiches, coffee, ginger beer and apple tarts they hashed out the colour of the rooms.

They might have saved themselves a whole day. Mr K had envisaged a white palate throughout, to enhance the natural ambiance of the house. The tone, the mood, he postulated, was for harmony with the natural light, the feeling of nature in the raw. No adornments, just naked, white, pure atmosphere.

'Pfft.' Enid said.

Mr K had no concept of life in the raw.

Naturally, Enid's final choices would need to be run by Mr V and Mr K. Jack sent a letter with a bit of wool, a baby's face washer, an embroidery thread, a petal, and a shaving of a pink pencil. There was a lengthy explanation on the shades, the curtains Enid had chosen and the colour of the easy chair cushions.

'No, no, NO!' Mr Vuoto threw his hands in the air. 'This will never do, no.' The last 'no' pretty emphatic. Torheit was to be a beacon of modernity. It was to be the future. Mr V had some bright design concepts. Usually furniture is made to the parameters of a normal human form. Somewhere to put your legs, your elbows and something to rest your back on. Simple concepts. Mr V threw them out as antiquated, outdated and not nearly expensive enough for a house like Torheit. A letter was dispatched with instructions to wait. V & K would see to everything.

'Is that so?'

'Yes Mr Brown. V & K feel Torheit should be innovative inside and out.' Jack said. 'Mr Vuoto is coming down with the designs and some furniture in a week or two.

'Is that right?'

'Yes, he has some innovative things.' What those things were Jack wasn't quite sure, but one thing was certain, Mr Brown was paying for them.

The first week was taken with painting everything white, as per Mr Ks instructions. It was a blinding white that was called arctic. The painter's pupils were like pin pricks at the end of the day as he washed his brushes and marvelled at the choice of colour, or lack thereof.

'A nice blue would go well,' he said to Jack.

'This is an icon Mr Du Bois.'

'Still, a bit o' colour would go well.'

Claude Du Bois liked a bit of colour. His mother often said he had an eye for colour.

'We're coloured people Claude, we like colour,' Mrs Du Bois often said, her one and only joke which was repeated ad nauseum.

Jack shaded his eyes to the white.

'It's called arctic.' Claude squinted.

'It's very white, isn't it.' Jack said.

'You're tellin' me.' Du Bois shook his head, the white splats on his face giving him a piebald look.

Parsnip Jones worked like a wind-up toy installing the kitchen sink. His quiet, methodical way put the wind up the Clutz clan as they watched him work.
'Alright there?' Skeet asked Parsnip.
'Yup.'
A few hours passed.
'All good Parsnip?' Winslow asked.
'Yup.'
The next morning the Clutz brothers were smoking and looking at the tidy way Parsnip worked. He just didn't seem to make a mess, and yet he got the job done. It was un-nerving. Down-right un-natural.
'What's up Parsnip?' Woodruff asked.
'Nothin'' Parsnip answered.
The man was a machine. He just worked and didn't complain, take a break, smoke or stop to chew the fat. He was a shining example of a work ethic. The Clutz brothers thought it best to steer clear of Parsnip lest his ethics be contagious. Vern would think they were sick or something if they actually worked a full day.
And so a week or two passed for Jack, keeping his mouth firmly shut with advice as Parsnip installed a kitchen sink, not mentioning the light fittings that found their way to the Golf club-house, keeping quiet about some reappropriated wood that found its way onto the Clutz dray, trying to fathom the calculations from Mr Clutz's quote to his ready reckoning and writing letters to Miss Hazel Brown.

Then, Mr Vuoto's telegram alerted Jack to his imminent arrival. After a hearty breakfast, Jack squeezed into his trousers, huffed his way to his motorbike and joggled his way to Torheit. Mrs Sweetwater's home cooking was taking it's inevitable toll on Jack's waistline. For a fellow accustomed to university meals of sandwiches and hot dogs, three squares a day was a pleasurable change, one Jack's waistline quite appreciated.

He rode his Harley Davidson on the new track to the front/back door and cut the engine. Looking down the slope it was quite a surprise to see Hazel at the wheel of her Aunt's Ford, Mr V and Mrs Parker sitting in the back.

'Hello,' Jack waved while Hazel pulled on the hand brake.

'Hello,' Mrs Parker waved as Jack bounded down to the Ford and held the door for his superior.

'A motor truck, it is coming no?'

"I hope so sir.'

The gang stood in the dirt and looked at Torheit.

'It is magnificent no?' No-one was actually waiting for Mr Ricardo Vuoto to eat his hat, but the offer still stood.

Hazel looked at Jack's stomach, 'quite remarkable,' she smirked. Jack sucked it in and tried to keep it there.

'It certainly is,' Mrs Parker answered Mr V. 'Reminds me of something, but I can't think what.'

Hazel proffered. 'An apple crate Aunt Jane?'

'That's it. An apple crate.' They all looked at the apple crate. 'Where's the front door?' Mrs Parker said.

'Round there,' Jack pointed up the rise. 'Torheit is made for the eye to run with the horizontal line. Nothing to disturb the symmetry.'

'Oh.' Mrs Parker nodded. 'Still, I like those,' she pointed to the numerous urns scatted about the place like skittles after a rowdy game.

'They're urns.'

'Yes.' Mrs Parker smiled while Hazel jabbed Jack in the ribs with her elbow and smirked.

'Oh. Right.'

There was a tooting of a klaxon and their admiration was interrupted by a motor truck making its slow, careful way up the track.

'Ah, furniture, no.'

'Yes.' Jack said.

Two burly men alighted and began to take the canvas off the back of the truck. Mr V fizzed about as his 'ideas' were unpacked and carried with great ceremony, up the rise and into Torheit.

'I must say, it's all very exciting isn't it?' Mrs Parker watched as they carried something inside. 'Mr Vuoto said I should come and take a look, for my museum you see.'

'Oh. Right.' Jack looked at something that might have been a chair being carried up the rise followed by Mr V.

'Oh look, there's my parents.' Hazel pointed to a trap making its way to the site.

'Thought we'd come and take a look.' Bill helped Enid down. There was a flurry of greetings and then Bill looked at a piece of furniture being heaved onto the shoulder of a fellow and making its way up to the front/back door.

'Mr Vuoto is here to supervise,' Jack said. 'Shall we go inside?'

Mr V was fussing over the placement of the furniture, but stood back to collect the accolades when he saw his audience.

'It is...no?'

There was silence as the crowd looked at modernity in all its glory.

Some of the furniture looked like packing crates. Bill sat down and shot back up. The chair, was designed to speak of elegance, sophistication and lightness, so Mr V said, but screamed back pain, and cut into the back of Bill's legs like a cane in grade school. Enid looked at another of Mr V's offerings. Her hips, hips that had born ten children and cooked countless meals, would not fit no matter how big the shoe horn.

Seats with rigid angles were described as 'sculptural'.

'Every object in the house has meaning, no, and a reason for being there.' Mr Vuoto struck a pose.

'I just wanna sit down.' Bill said getting, quite neatly, to the nub of the thing.

Hazel and Aunt Jane tried a settee that was so uncomfortable it threw anyone who dare sit in it to the floor. Jack came to the rescue and pulled the women to their feet as they began to laugh.

'It embody the concept of sculptural movement, no,' Mr V said.

'Well, I don't know about that.' Bill put his hands on his hips and shook his head.

'Er, Mr Vuoto, do you have our bed?' Enid asked, hoping it might make things right.

'Si,' Mr V jumped at the chance to show off his prize. It looked like a normal bed which, considering the chairs, was a good start. It looked like something one could get comfortable in.

'Try no?'

'Oh,' Enid inched forward and sat on the edge of the mattress. She bounced a little, then a lot.

'It's so soft.'

'Here, let me try.' Bill sat on the other side and gave it the bounce test.

'It is the modern. The springs you see, no?'

'Springs.'

'Si.' Mr V took his shoes off and hopped on the bed and laid down. 'Springs.'

Aunt Jane sat down and bounced. Hazel sat next to her father and bounced.

'Is good no? The Marshall Coil. Si. Individually pocket coil spring no?'.

'It's very good.' Bill took his shoes off and made himself comfortable.

'Jack, come and sit down,' Hazel patted the bed.

'No, really I couldn't.' There was something uncomfortable about sharing a bed with your superior, two old married people, the girl you quite liked and her aunt.

'Come on,' Hazel coaxed.

'No. I don't think so.' Jack backed out of the room and into Noel Braithwaite.

'Sorry, did I interrupt something?' Braithwaite took a look at the romping on the big bed.

'Oh, no. Marshall coils you know.'

'Fancy.' Braithwaite said and pulled out a pencil

and pad. 'Noel Braithwaite. From the press. Do you remember me?'

'Yes.' Jack had read the satirical piece from Braithwaite. He didn't like the man.

'Thought I'd just pop down, see what's what.'

Jack closed the bedroom door, 'see what's what eh?'

'Yes, that's the idea.' Braithwaite tried to bluster his way through the cold reception.

'I read your piece Mr Braithwaite. I didn't much care for it.'

'No?'

'No.'

'Just trying to make a buck Mr Renfrew. Just trying to make a buck like you.'

'Really? At other people's expense?'

'News one day, bottom of the bird cage the next. People have short memories Mr Renfrew, very short.'

This revelation wasn't what Jack wanted to hear. He was hoping for a bit of immortality himself in regard to Torheit, his name forever associated with the build.

'So now you're looking for another scathing piece?'

'Oh no. My editor wants updates. He's a bit of a modernist type of guy. Loves this stuff.' Braithwaite waved his pencil at the furniture, the rooms.

'Ah.'

'So if I could just have a few words?'

'Well,' Jack began when Mr V and the bed hoppers came out the door.

'Mr Vuoto,' Jack introduced Mr Braithwaite, 'from the press.'

'Ah, the press.' Mr V grabbed Braithwaite's arm and steered him to the settee. After they scrabbled up from the floor, Mr V threw his finger in the air and began.

The audience watched the performance as Mr V said, 'embody the concept, no, of sculptural movement. Si!' He went on with 'combines traditional elementals with innovative materials, no'

Then there was 'cantilever style.' One simply must have a cantilever; Huxley's words came back as an echo.

Mr V talked about the 'starkness of the form' while he strutted his form for the press.

'What about comfort,' Bill asked.

'An irrelevance,' Mr V waved his hand in the air. He sat bolt upright in his 'modern sculptured chair' with a pained yet satisfied look and might have used the word 'ergonomic'—although he'd need to wait forty years to get that opportunity, (it was first penned in 1950).

'And you think this is the future, Mr Vuoto?' Noel Braithwaite tried to sit in a chair that cut the circulation from his legs.

'Si.' Mr V went to lean back and felt the cantilever begin to topple, so remained upright by holding onto the arms of his 'chair' and leaning forward as if 100 years old and hard of hearing.

'So,' Braithwaite said, 'people will clamber for this—stuff?'

'Si.' Mr V hung on—to the concept and the chair, both having the propensity to cast him off at the earliest opportunity. 'This is a manifesto of interpretations, no?'

It all sounded a bit too grand for farmer Brown and in fact later interpreters would wonder at the contrivance of steel, leather and the lack of comfort.

Mr Braithwaite didn't need to wonder. He had all the words he needed to make a story, that it was a truthful account, a bonus.

The gang watched the dining chairs come in two by two, their leather slung seats looking like old men's jowls. They were tubular and low backed affairs which crunched your lower lumber into a cantilever that might need a rack to straighten out. Luckily the modern take on the chaise lounge looked like it might just do the trick, made of steel and designed to pull your spine straight up through the base of your skull.

'Isn't it very modern,' Mrs Parker said as they placed the chaise lounge in the front room.

'Si, modern.' Mr V nodded.

The group were distracted by the ruckus at the front/back door as the delivery men swore, cursed and cussed.

'Eh?' Bill went to investigate.

'Won't go mister.'

And that was about the size of it. And an extra ordinarily large size it was too.

I don't know about you, but when there is furniture to move, everyone is an expert and everyone has an idea. Now with nine people in attendance, the opportunities to add ones two cents worth were almost limitless.

The round dining table, made of one piece of concrete and polished to a fabulous shine had a diameter which Sisyphus might recognise. He was the poor fellow who cheated death twice and was punished by giving him a boulder to push uphill for eternity. The dining table might not have been a boulder or eternal punishment, but it sure felt like it.

'If you just lean it to the left,' someone suggested.

'If you could twist it as you push,' a voice said.

'What if you try to roll it and then flick it a bit.' Physics dictates what will and will not fit, but that didn't stop the suggestions.

'How about if someone stands on one side, someone stands on the other and you just sort of push.' One can convey so much with an eye roll. The delivery men gave an eye roll that was practically an essay in 'if I hear one more stupid suggestion...' Delivery men have nerves of steel when it comes to suggestions. They are quite accustomed to 'helpful' suggestions and usually ignore most of them. After all they have been doing this job for quite some time.

'It won't go.' The young man said and he looked long and hard at Mr V. He was probably thinking that only an idiot would design something that couldn't fit through a door. If he had his way, everything would come ready to assemble on the spot. It was an idea that like Mr Vs ergonomics would need to wait forty years and be called flat-pack.

'Can you just...' Mr V began.

'When pigs fly mister.'

'Ah.' It wasn't much of an opinion, but Mr V felt genius absolved him from the practical, the applied every-day minutiae.

Enid took a long look at the problem. She studied it from every angle and then said, 'take it away.' Problem solved.

'We have a perfectly nice dining table at the farm. It's legs come off for transport, it was my mother's and it will fit. Women sometimes have a way to cut through to the heart of the problem and although much maligned, mainly by the opposite sex, they get the job done.

'So, um, what do you want us to do with this,' said the young man holding one side of the disc.

'Well,' Mr Clutz came in on the problem, 'I might know a fella.'

Mayor Wynkoop wasn't one to look a gift horse in the mouth. In fact he didn't look too hard at all at the knock down prices (or so he thought) of the furniture that came his way. To have modern, up to the minute, V & K furniture was more than he could hope for in his Golf club. Bill, via Vern Clutz shifted all his spatial concept furniture except the bed to the Mayor. The provenance of the pieces was a Clutz work of fiction. Bill got his money, Vern got the profit and the Mayor quite a bit of kudos. Of course being totally impractical to sit in and on, the patrons and captains of industry could be seen on any day lounging on the lawn furniture in all weathers, such is the nature of comfort over fashion.

'Now, this is better,' Bill sank into his comfy chair that had been transported from the farm. It didn't quite fit the stark décor of the lounge room, nor did it fit the vast dimensions of the room, but it fitted Bill's derriere like a glove. When Enid's chair arrived and was placed opposite Bill's by the fireplace Torheit became more than a brown apple crate, it became a home. They did keep the settee though, as it was quite a talking point and great fun when some unsuspecting visitor was invited to take a seat.

It might be years down the track, but one day, some bright spark might find the original drawings of the furniture and their placement, put two and two together and reunite the iconic Torheit with its gloriously modern, uncomfortable furniture, but that would be a long time coming.

CHAPTER 22

Noel Braithwaite of the City Morning Daily might not have been directly responsible for the avalanche of salesmen, but Bill and Enid had to blame someone, and he was the likely candidate. Once his article hit the husting spouting 'modern appliances for a modern woman', various salesmen found their way to Torheit. How they acquired the address could be directly attributed to Mr Braithwaite, because a daily paper thrives on advertising, and well... it's a perfect match for a patented shoe polisher and a quarter page spread on page seven.

'Now Mrs Brown, Enid if I may—just plug this wonderful, amazing iron in to your socket and you're bound to get a shock—it's so easy. Enid looked at the wires attached to the electric terminals and thought it quite likely she would get quite a shock.

'The Electric Heating and Manufacturing Company of Los Angeles stand by their product Mrs Brown.' The salesman put on the hard sell, although this iron was in the nature of a free trial.

'In case of a burn out on the wires,' and he pointed to the terminals, which were exposed, 'why, all you need Mrs Brown is a screwdriver and it's a two minute job.'

'Really?'

'Oh yes. Easy. And to show our absolute trust in our iron we have included two wire cables. One for the light fitting and one for your wall sockets.'

'Fancy that.'

'You do have electricity night and day I hope?'

'I couldn't say.' Enid shrugged.

'Well, our wires will see you right Mrs Brown. Never fear, the Electric Heating and Manufacturing Company is here.'

And if you are wondering what the heck the salesman was blathering on about, in the tradition of Americans making a buck, the electrical companies including Zennith Union Electrification Company, only supplied electricity to houses after the sun went down. Who needs lights on in the day for heaven's sake. Well the housewife thought she might. How can you iron at night without a light, because you need the same source of electrification aka light fitting.

So some bright spark suggested if they supplied electricity in the day as well, they could double their revenue. Good ol' American know how spelt with a capital $. It was a turning point in electrical appliances in the home as Enid found out.

The fellow espousing the two prong socket was

first through the door of Torheit.

'No more lamp plugs, Mrs B. Modern up to the minute sockets. Two pronged sockets Mrs B.'

Parchmore was summoned. He installed one in every room, the two pronged man wasn't going as far as giving more than one room each for free.

Enid looked at the booty she was collecting.

'Electrification is the future Mrs Brown,' the iron man said. Enid had read electricity was the saviour for people losing their wits and at the other end of the scale—death.

'Why, just look at the way it glides. No more heaving an iron full of hot coals. No more hard work.'

Enid looked at the fellow. Did he really know what hard work entailed. Had he had ten children—all who needed their clothes ironed. She doubted it.

'If you just try it Mrs Brown—Enid, and give us your humble opinion.'

And so it was with the electric hair-curler, the electric washing machine et al.

The sales men descended like locusts or manna from heaven—it all depended on how you looked at the gift horse. From brooms to hair pins, roasting pans to things that suck the dirt right off the floor. Enid and Bill were sucked in.

Every day someone was knocking on the front door of Torheit—once they found it of course.

It was all very flattering, exciting and free.

'Mrs Brown your life wouldn't be complete without a new fangles doo-dad.' It seemed there was a man inventing a new doo-dad every week, and apparently Mrs Enid Brown of Brownsville needed one, or sometimes two.

Then there were the slicker purveyors of household items. These men had the patter, the persuasion, the perseverance. Bed linen, tea towels, wooden spoons and meat grinders. And all they required of Enid Brown was a word or two from a home spun homebody farmer's wife.

Enid soon ran out of superlatives.

'Nice.'

'Quite nice.'

'Very nice.'

'Really very nice.'

Copywriter and ad men, however hardboiled, however jaded, can only make so much out of 'nice'.

'Did you really say that Edie?' Bill asked as he read the advert for Bald Eagle ~curl-o-matic. Obviously it was named by a man who had no idea on marketing, however patriotic.

'I wouldn't be without my Bald Eagle curl-o-matic. It's so nice!' It didn't sound like something Enid would say, but with all the goings on, Bill wasn't so sure.

They read about sheets and pillow cases from Manchester, Ohio, a happy co-incidence of names, that they apparently endorsed.

Pillows from Rochard Texas, (some wag thought it would be funny to add a hyphen, Roc-hard the result), on which the Browns evidently slept like babies.

Buffalo Brooms, Myrtle May hair pins and the magical Hoover pneumatic vacuum cleaner -which sucks the dirt...well we all know what it does by now!

'Did you honestly say that mother?' Hazel wrote in her weekly letter. She'd cut out the advertisement and posted it.

'The latest thing in electrification of your home. Why? I wouldn't be without it.' SAYS MRS BROWN. Enid felt the folded letter in her pocket and looked at the booty collecting on the kitchen table.

'Edie, you need to be strong. You don't necessarily need to say yes to everything. Look at all this stuff.' Bill swept his hands over the pile of free goods.

'Well they say it's for free, and they are so nice and polite,' Enid said, stroking her meat grinder.

'Well, I'm going to put my foot down Edie. No more gadgets or do-hickeys.'

'Yes Bill.' Enid was hoping for an electric frypan with a new do-dad called a therm-o-stat.

Bill, being made of sterner stuff was flattered with Bathadora soap powder - perfumed, no less! and razor blades for the discerning gentleman's bathroom routine, but he only took them under sufferance.

And then a stout gentleman came calling from the Gutfeldt weight reducing belt manufacturing company.

'Mr Gutfeldt at your service Mr Brown.'

'Oh. Hello.' Bill shook the man's hand.

'Oh my giddy aunt,' Enid looked at the large box Mr Gutfeldt placed on the floor with lurid pictures of svelte men in athletic poses plastered on the sides.

'I have what you need, Mr Brown.'

'Ya don't say.'

'I do say.' Mr Gutfeldt extolled the virtues of a flat stomach, although himself not the best advert for the product. As fat Dutchmen go he was on the top rung. Mr Gutfeldt hitched up his trousers, and went into his lengthy spiel on the benefits, the ease of operation, the modern man and his stomach.

Bill listened and took it all in. He began to envisage his stomach like a washboard. He began to think he was twenty one again.

'You know it's my wife's fault,' Bill said. 'She keeps feeding me.'

The men looked at Enid as if she had a funnel in one hand and a ham hock in the other.

'Bill.' Enid huffed. Mr Gutfeldt continued, throwing a contemptuous look in Enid's direction.

'And Mr Brown, I am here to make your life complete. With just a word or two on how much you have benefited from the Gutfeldt weight reducing belt, you can have this Gutfeldt weight reducing belt absolutely free.'

'No?' Really?'

Mr Gutfeldt nodded. 'Shall I give you a demonstration?'

'Bill Brown,' Enid said with a large dose of indignation.

The men disappeared into the Gentlemen's bathroom for quite some time. When they re-appeared Bill had a smile on his face and Mr Gutfeldt was slapping him on the back.

'Marvellous. Simply Marvellous,' Bill said as he sucked in his belly which a Hoover pneumatic vacuum cleaner might have stalled on.

It doesn't take long for something new, exciting and modern to become passé, old and tired. Such is the fickle nature of advertising. One minute you can't make enough of your Bald Eagle ~curl-o-matics and the next everyone wants straight hair. And to be fair Mrs Browns endorsements were wearing thin, in contrast to Bill's stomach, despite his administration of the Gutfeldt weight reducing belt.

But, amid all the falderol, the hoo-ha, there was a much bigger prize on offer. V & K were angling for the Bossart Award for Architectural Excellence.

The Bossart was a big deal. Mr K knew his reputation would be enhanced to such a degree he might possibly see a marble bust of his noggin in the hall of fame for architects.

And to get this accolade there was the necessity of the judges visiting the candidates work of genius.

Jack felt like he'd swallowed Mrs Sweetwater's soft boiled egg all over again when he read the urgent telegram from Huxley.

K VISIT FRI IMMINENT STOP BOSSART WIGS IN ATTENDANCE STOP SPIT AND POLISH STOP DON'T PANIC SLAVES ON WAY WED STOP

Jack panicked. Not only his boss, but the judges, and the lads from the dungeon. If he was going down in flames he would have a large audience.

Torheit began to look like a home. Enid and Bill had installed their homespun farm furniture, they had hung a few pictures and with their fine new appliances were beginning to settle in. The new stove had stopped smoking, the Orlando Woodrow Automatic electric washer had done its first load and Enid had just pulled a first loaf of bread from the oven as Bill poured a cup of coffee when Jack burst through the back/front door and surveyed the scene of domestic bliss.

'No, no, no,' he pulled at his hair and spun around to see some of Bill's long underwear hanging in front of the stove.

'Coffee son?'

'Mr Brown,' Jack looked around at the comforts of country living. Shoes on newspaper in front of the stove, underwear drying, tea towels and comfortable furniture as far as the eye could see. He flopped down into a comfy chair by the fire and held his head in his hands, his elbows on his knees.

'Are you alright Jack?' Enid came over with a fresh baked biscuit and a cup of coffee.

'Mrs Brown,' Jack began, 'I...' he couldn't get out words. Words that might describe his unemployment and his prospects of never working again. Once Mr K and the judges saw this scene of domesticity, all the furniture of Mr Vs gone, and the vision of Torheit adulterated into normal everyday domestic bliss, he knew his life was over. He might as well go back to beet farming. The thought of beets made him shudder,

'Are you cold? Sit closer to the fire Jack.' Enid edged Jack forward.

'Mrs Brown,' Jack looked at Enid with pleading eyes.

'Yes?'

'I'm in a bit of a pickle.'

CHAPTER 23

Jack hadn't been sitting still as the Browns moved in and made Torheit a home. There was the matter of the steps to the back/front door, the landscaping around the house, the disposal of rubbish, the endless pilfering from the Clutz clan and to top the whole shebang off, Freelan Quill had issued a warrant concerning the knob-and-tube electricity. Apparently there needed to be more knobs and less tubes to comply with some stupid new-fangled regulation that the planning department had just thought up while eating breakfast. Mr Parchmore was busy at the Golf Club and couldn't be contacted. The mention of Quill made Jack's lip curl.

'So, what's the problem son?' Bill put down his catalogue and sat back with his biscuit then wiggled his socked toes in front of the fire grate.

Where do you start?

'Well,' Jack took a deep breath.

Bill nodded, 'furniture.'

Enid tisked, 'Award'.

Bill frowned, 'Judges.'

Enid shook her head, 'Friday.'

Everyone narrowed their eyes at the mention of Mr Quill.

'So, that's about it. I lose my job, Torheit is relegated to just another building, you quite probably will need to give back the free things and...' Jack shrugged, 'fhttt,' he snapped his fingers. 'Gone.'

'Right.' Bill brushed his shirt front of biscuit crumbs and winked at Jack. 'Mother likes to use her Hoover,' he pointed to the floor.

'My Hoover?' Enid asked.

'Hmmm,' Jack nodded. 'Quite possibly.'

'Oh my.' Enid bit her bottom lip. 'Oh my word.'

'And when are we expecting company?'

'Any time soon Mr Brown.' Jack brought out the telegram and read it through once more.

'Wednesday, that's today.'

'Sure is son.'

'If they left first thing, well the train...' Jack didn't get any further as there was a honk from a klaxon and the unmistakable sound of an engine.

'Oh, my giddy aunt,' Enid looked out of the window, 'it's our Hazel and some young men.'

'What?' Jack jumped up and looked out of the long window.

'It's...' it's...my friends.'

'I'll put the kettle on.' Enid began to get cracking on that famous country hospitality as Jack scooted outside and down the newly minted steps at the side of the house.

'Hello there,' he bounded over to the car, hoping for a miracle with the apprentices arrival. His high-spirits were short lived as just at the wrong time Mr Quill had come out to Torheit to have another go at making Jack's life a misery. Just by breathing Freelan Quill had perfected the knack. Jack rolled his eyes at the man on the bicycle trundling up the track.

'Who's that?' Putney asked as he heard Jack groan.

'That,' Hazel said as she took off her driving gloves, is Mr Freelan Quill, Steerforth's County Planning Officer—and quite a big pain in the neck.

'Really?' Swindon watched Quill hop off his bicycle and survey the going's on.

Putney adjusted his spectacles and said, 'He's coming this way.'

'Come on, let's go inside,' Jack held the door for Hazel and the young men followed.

The lads oohed and ahhed at Torheit while being hustled inside. They rubbernecked at the bricks,

'I didn't realise they were so...so...brown'

They regarded the urns,

'They are, well they are everywhere.'

And staring at the slit windows in relation to the horizontal lines,

'They really do draw the eye don't they.'

Jack shooed the apprentices up the steps.

'Mr Quill, I think you will find Mr Clutz over yonder burning things and Mr Parchmore is at the club,' Jack yelled and sprinted up the steps to the front/back door, checked everyone was accounted for and shut it, bolted it and smiled.

'Everyone rushed to the windows and looked

out for Quill. Freelan was trudging over to a bonfire, dodging the horse soil improver, the mud and rocks.

'Well, what have we here?' Enid began setting out cups and saucers, biscuits and cake.

The story over tea and cake began with Huxley, as all things usually do. He had heard the rumour of the Bossart Award, the imminent arrival and had the foresight to put two and two together.

'He came around to see Aunt Jane and charmed the socks off her.' Hazel said. 'I'm getting paid father, a chauffeur's wage.'

'Fancy that. My daughter a chauffeur.' Bill puffed his chest out just a little.

'Yes, Huxley wheedled a few days in the field for us,' Steinbeck said. 'We are the draughtsmen Mrs Brown.'

'Oh.'

'I did the urns Mrs Brown,' Putney said spooning sugar into his tea.

'Fancy that.'

When Mr V said the lads should get themselves to Torheit and acquaint themselves with the work before the judges arrived, everyone knew it was at Huxley's instigation. No-one had actually broached the subject of the nature of the charabanc. Educational exercise or work related—one was polony sandwiches the other attracting one day's pay.

'So where is Mr Huxley?' Bill asked.

'Oh, he's been seconded into chauffeur for Mr V and Mr K,' Swindon said helping himself to a biscuit. In fact Mr V and Mr K had taken quite a liking to the Pierce-Arrow 66 and high society, plus the circles Huxley III frequented—although Huxley had a sneaking suspicion it was his aunt Lydia Huxley-Croaker's luncheons that really hit the spot.

It was turning into quite the convivial morning tea, when there was a loud knock on the bolted door. Conversation stopped as they listened.

'I know you're in there Mr Renfrew, I'll be back.' They all watched a sheaf of paper slide under the door. 'Twenty days or you will be in breach,' Quill said to the front/back door.

Enid watched Quill bicycle away, 'he's gone,' and everyone could breathe once again.

'What's all that about?'

'Well,' Jack began and didn't finish until he'd exhausted the subject of knobs and tubes.

'Ah.' Steinbeck nodded, 'I know a fellow who just might be able to fix your knobs and tubes issues Renfrew. I just need to send a telegram.'

And so Hazel and Steinbeck were on a mission. That mission was to telegram Steinbeck's second cousin on his mother's side who just happened to be related to Thomas Edison the inventor of all societies wonders and woes. Timothy Edison carried his relatives initials and a sizable debt, so he could be bought just like any electrical appliance and would sign anything, given the right incentive... around eight dollars was the going rate.

'I think it might just impress your Mr Quill,' Steinbeck said as they drove away from Torheit and a soon to be flurry of activity.

'So, Renfrew, what's the problem, besides Mr Quill?' Putney asked polishing off a second cup of tea and a third slice of cake.

'Well,' Jack looked around at the kitchen. 'It's like this...' And what transpired was a logistical nightmare that would need to be accomplished in one day. 'and the Mayor must never know.'

'Right.' Bill stood up and brushed some more crumbs on the floor. 'Mrs Brown just loves her Hoover,' he said.

How many people does it take to strip out a house of comfortable furniture and replace it with modern, back-cracking monstrosities? As many as you can muster, plus a few tractors, horse and carts, traps, automobiles, trolleys and drays.

The trick was to do it all in secret. Not an easy feat when you live in a small town called Brownsville where everyone knows everything about everyone.

'Should we do it in the dark?' Putney asked.

'Too hard.'

'What about at the crack of dawn?' Swindon offered.

It sounded like an idea, a good one for a change.

And so the afternoon was productively spent gathering helping hands (having a gaggle of children is certainly an advantage sometimes), collecting harnesses and horses, traps and tarps.

ଓଃ

The apprentices were dispatched to the Brown's farmhouse for the night. They were treated to mountains of stew and dumplings, feather quilts and hospitality that makes you think farmers really are the salt of the earth.

Jack was in two minds about telling Mrs Sweetwater. Although another of those salt of the earth types she did have a tendency to blather. On the other hand, if she was roped into making tea and cakes, then they might keep an eye on her gossipy ways.

Over a dinner of chicken pie Jack outlined Mrs Sweetwater's vital part in the chicanery. He emphasised her need for discretion, his confidence that she could keep a secret, introducing one upmanship in the form of 'not like Mrs Delany', and finally Mrs Sweetwater's wonderful cake making abilities.

'I'll do it.' Clara Sweetwater brought out a peach cobbler. 'Mrs Delany didn't hear it from me.'

But as we were to find out later, Mrs Delany did hear it from someone, and then it was about as much a clandestine operation as a thirteen gun salute on the fourth of July.

γ

Jack took a trip after his evening meal, to the farm house with a few bottles of beer. Five bottles of beer wasn't going to go far when there was a lot of catching up to do, and so the Brown brothers, Bill and Parsnip showed the city slickers just what homespun hospitality really entailed with whisky, cider and home-made cherry liqueur, all sloshed down with some boiled peanuts. It was quite a party, even Parsnip Jones was coaxed into telling a grand tale about the Governor's u bend, a small dog and a gold ring that had everyone in stitches. Though, to be fair after a bottle of cherry liqueur and home brewed cider which might or might not be as proof as rubbing alcohol, everything was hilarious.

Steinbeck thought the Brown girls simply wonderful. Putney eulogised on the marvellous fresh air, just before he passed out. Swindon wondered if he should have a career change and marry a farmer's daughter, until Jack pointed out that he thought of it first. The assembled company looked at Hazel who was sipping cherry liqueur.

'What?'

The crowd looked at Jack, who smiled and fell off his stool.

'Oh no. No. NO!' Hazel said as the penny dropped.

David Brown nudged Swindon, who hoiked Jack to his knees.

'Grrrrh...' Jack made a noise like a blocked drain and giggled. 'Hazel,' Jack said from his kneeling position, 'Would you...?'

'Jack Renfrew, don't you dare.' Hazel blushed.

'Would you—if I asked, would you,' Jack looked up at Hazel and smiled.

The Browns looked on. Steinbeck jabbed Jack in the ribs with the fire poker.

'What I'm trying to say,' Jack began again but under the influence of drink he didn't quite know what he was proposing, although that's exactly what he was proposing.

'Son?'

'Mr Brown, salt of the earth.' Jack scrambled up and slapped Mr Brown on the back.

'Hazel,' Jack came over all dreamy and then quite out of character grabbed the young lady and planted a kiss on her lips. She didn't resist and there was a rousing cheer to be heard in the Brown farmhouse. Everyone had had more than enough alcohol to swear Jack had asked and Hazel had accepted. Although in the cold light of day, there might have been the odd moment when no-one could absolutely, hand on heart say they remembered the moment. Home-made, triple strength cherry liqueur has that effect.

What everyone could say with certainty was, as hang-overs go, triple strength home-made cherry liqueur packed a punch when it came to the morning after.

It wasn't the best of mornings to be lugging furniture from Torheit to the farmhouse, and bring furniture from the Golf Club to Torheit. Despite a thumping head, Jack delegated and controlled the traffic.

'Can I keep the picture of my...?' Enid asked.

'No.'

'Can we put this rug...?'

'No.'

'What about?'

'NO!'

And so it went. There was a look-out posted at the turnoff, Parsnip Jones had the keys to the club house and was in charge of pilfering the furniture and Jack organised the placement of Mr Vs conceptualization of modernisation with sculptural overtones.

Steinbeck, Swindon and Putney, although the worse for farming hospitality, managed to put away a full breakfast for the task ahead. They humped, lugged and heaved the comfortable chairs, sofas, chaise lounges and foot stalls out to the dray and did it all again at the farmhouse. If there is one thing to set your metabolism right when in the grip of hangover it is sweating it out. The apprentices sweated as they exerted their underused muscles. The saving grace was the promise of Mrs Sweetwater's muffins at morning tea.

Bill, Parsnip and several of the Brown boys were busy loading the cart at the club, which in the scheme of things was easy peasy. All the furniture was either cubed or oblong so with a bit of jiggling it stacked like a child's wooden puzzle.

'And you actually sit on this?' Parsnip asked.

'Well,' Bill scratched his head. 'It's modern.'

'Is that what you call it.' Parsnip threw a rope over the pile and tied it down.

Even if you start at the crack of dawn, it is nigh on impossible to evade detection.

'What's all this then?' Vern Clutz asked as he drove his dray up the track to Torheit.

'What's all this,' Skeet echoed.

Jack stopped from carrying a drying frame with Bill's shirts still pegged on it, 'ah.'

'He says, ah pa.'

'That he did son.' Vern tied the reins of his faithful horse and hopped down from the dray. 'We came over to finish up on the roof. Brown said, 'twas leaking.'

'Look, Mr Clutz, we are in a bit of a pickle.' Jack said.

'What Mr Renfrew is trying to say Mr Clutz,' Hazel butted in with her mother's sewing box under her arm, 'is that we are moving my parent's furniture out for a rather important assessment, and possibly an award, and replacing it with the intended furniture to better enhance the conceptualization of modernisation with sculptural overtones.' Jack looked at Hazel. She really was one heck of a gal.

'Overtones pa,' Skeet said.

'Is that right.'

'It is. Now if you would be so kind, we are in a bit of a hurry.' Hazel walked past Clutz then turned and winked at Jack before heading to the automobile to relieve herself of her load.

'An award eh?'

'Yes. And I was wondering would it be to your liking to call you Clutz & sons Builders in the final analysis for the award, or just Mr Clutz, Builder?'

'Well...'

'Pa?'

'& sons. Er...will there be some sort of prize money or the like?'

'Quite possibly Mr Clutz, quite possibly.' Jack waited for the fish to come in.

'So...'

'Yes?'

'Do ya need any help?'

'Well... we could do with an extra dray. You see those book cases,' Jack pointed up the rise, 'they need to go over to the farmhouse.'

'Right you are.' Mr Clutz spat and pulled up his trousers. 'We'll do this and then get on the roof and have a look. I can't see it leaking myself, but we'll take a look. Looks like it might rain.'

'Rain.' Skeet looked at the sky.

'Perhaps you should look at the roof first Mr Clutz.'

'If ya sure ya can manage.'

'Oh, yes...and by the way, we don't want the Mayor...' Jack waved his hands over the proceedings.

'Right you are,' Vern spat and winked.

'Pa?'

'Never you mind son, never you mind.'

⌇

Conceptualized modern furniture can be quite heavy and although cube, oblong and rectangle it doesn't lend itself to getting in doorways with a minimum of fuss. It's especially difficult when you have someone pushing, someone pulling and a third giving expert advice. Tempers can get frayed and on top of a hangover its practically a perfect storm.

'Will you just get out of the way.' David Brown shoved Skeet Clutz who shoved back.

'Ya couldn't pull the skin off a rice pudding,' Skeet said by way of an insult.

'You couldn't open an umbrella even if it was spring loaded.'

Country folk have a unique way with slurs.

'Please,' Jack said trying to get things through the door without fuss, 'we are on a timeline here.'

'Not my fault this haystack is in need of a pitchfork.' David said.

Jack and David looked at Skeet as he processed the insult.

'Skeet,' Hazel came to the rescue, 'I really need your help over here.' Skeet squeezed past David and gave a huff, then said, 'some of us got work to do. Better go back to ya knitting.' It was a persistent rumour since school days that the Brown brothers, surrounded by sisters sat around at night and knitted. What Skeet didn't know was that sea

Captains, sailors and all manner of 'he' men knitted and had done since someone found two sticks and a lazy afternoon in their schedule.

The jibe made David grit his teeth and in a moment of sheer bullish determination he lifted the heavy table on his shoulder and carried it into the house then plopped it down in the kitchen.

'Knitting. Pfft.'

As the modern pieces reappeared Jack fussed over their placement, trying to remember where all the cubes fitted in relation to the rhomboids and the rectangles.

'Didn't it go there,' Bill said.

'Ae you sure?'

'I don't really think it matters, do you?' Enid said as she put a cross-stitch cushion on a cantilever chair. Jack whipped it off just as quick, 'I think we need Torheit to look...well to look like it's not lived in.'

'Really?' Hazel frowned as she and Skeet set a bench down near the fireplace. 'Is it, this award, really such a big thing? I've never heard of it.'

Jack looked at her like she had just asked if being the President of the United States was a proper job. (That debate is for another time!)

'Right.' Hazel raised her eye brows and rolled her eyes.

'Now, you two,' Enid said, 'behave.' She smiled at Hazel and then smiled at Jack and at that moment the previous evenings events flashed past Jack and he took a deep breath and closed his eyes. He was sure he didn't say, or do anything that might redesign his future. He remembered asking Hazel if she would...something, but didn't remember what.

It might have been drive him to Timbuktu or sew on a button. He was not sure she actually said she would, but he did know, well, he was fairly certain he acted with the upmost decorum and manners. 'Good manners will never go astray' his mother often said.

'Mother,' Hazel blushed and looked over to Jack. 'We're not fighting.'

'I hope not. Not a very good start.'

'Mother, please.'

'Just saying Hazel, just saying.' Enid took her cushion and put it back on the chair.

'I...I...' Jack made his signature blocked drain noise. 'We...that is to say, I...well, I think we should get on, don't you?'

'Yes.' Hazel smiled at Skeet who had followed the conversation, but not understood one word.

'I think there was an occasional table over there,' Hazel pointed to a low windowsill.

'Er Hazel,' Jack pulled her aside, 'I just want you to know that...well, I think we all had a little too much last night and although I might have said things, I mean everything I said, whatever that was.'

'Oh.' Hazel frowned.

'Renfrew,' Swindon came bounding over with a vase, 'sorry to interrupt,' he winked, 'but this is the last load. We've done it.'

Jack looked around the main room. There were only a few pieces to place.

'Marvellous.'

'I'll leave you two love birds alone.' Swindon put his vase down on the mantel-piece and then had only one thing on his mind. Muffins.

Jack and Hazel stood and looked at the retreating Swindon, the words 'love birds' fluttering between them.

CHAPTER 24

'So, don't touch anything. Just hover if you can.' Jack flitted around Torheit, putting the final touches to the house. He picked up Enid's cushion, couldn't find anywhere to put it and placed it back on the cantilever chair.

'Are you coming back to the farmhouse Jack?' Hazel picked up the cushion and fluffed it.

'Huh?'

'Are you coming back home? Grandma Sweetwater has made quite an effort for our evening meal.'

'Oh, yes,' Jack smiled. Hazel was looking really quite delightful in the slant of the late afternoon sun.

'Well? Shall we go?' Hazel fussed with her hair, licked her lips and put her hands in the pockets of her overalls.

'Yes. Go.' Jack took one last look and as they walked out the door, Hazel bending down to pick a bit of grass from the floor.

'You know Mother really likes her Hoover.'

'Well, let's hope she gets to enjoy it,' Jack said, adding, 'because if this,' he waved his arms at Torheit, 'doesn't get some sort of accolade, the free samples just might come with strings attached.'

'Fingers crossed then.' Hazel crossed her fingers behind her back.

'Fingers crossed.' Jack looked up at the ceiling in an attitude of prayer, hoping it wouldn't rain. Mr Clutz had been busy all afternoon with felt, tar and paper.

And sometime in the early evening it began to rain; although the crowd at the Brown's farmhouse were too busy with big servings of beef stew and dumplings, big helpings of bread and butter and gallons of hot tea to notice.

Jack sat next to Hazel and talked of goldfish, sports, motorbikes and the intimate workings of the combustion engine, but didn't mention the elephant in the room. Hazel Brown listened to it all. She added her knowledge of early planting, how to roll a hay bale, what to put in sheep dip for ticks and the temperature needed for sourdough bread, but there was no mention of a question asked or an answer given.

Steinbeck, Putney and Swindon ate their weight in scones, jam and cream and declared the country the only place where civilization was in evidence.

'The cradle of civilization,' Putney said stuffing another scone in his mouth.

'Salt of the earth,' Swindon added.

'If this is living, count me in,' Steinbeck said. There was a rousing cheer. The mission had been accomplished, the ruse was afoot and as far as the assembled company knew, Mayor Wynkoop was none the wiser.

As we mentioned, politicians are usually the last to know—and it wasn't until the Friday morning Mayor Wynkoop got wind of an impending visit by some important persons of consequence—big-wigs to the man in the street, and a reporter from the city morning paper, Noel Braithwaite, who had little truck for self-aggrandizement and affectation.

And how did the Mayor sense the change in the wind?

Brownsville is a small town. Skeet blabbed to Woodruff, who mentioned it to Dolan Delany and well—once the news was in the Delany household, there was nothing stopping it becoming common knowledge.

The morning dawned with clear skies, a few fluffy white clouds and a slight breeze. As the apprentices looked out of the window, smelt the bacon frying, the bread toasting and the coffee brewing, it looked like a perfect day.

Jack looked from his window at the sky. It promised to be a perfect day. Mrs Sweetwater brought in his coffee and toast.

'Really, Mrs Sweetwater, you spoil me.'

'Oh, you're practically family now Jack,' she winked.

The thought of being practically family had Jack's toast turning to ashes in his mouth. Not that there was anything wrong with being a Brown, but

273

the whole Hazel Brown question had his stomach in knots. He wasn't quite sure he had asked and he was even less sure she had said yes, although everyone else was jumping to conclusions like it was a George Herrington spring stilts convention. (FYI, dear George in 1891 invented a sort of pogo stick stilt with springs in them to catapult the wearer into the air. So unsound, they soon fell out of favour, probably after someone broke their neck.)

Jack's first stop was to the telegraph office. If there was anything untoward happening, he wanted to be the first to know.

Huxley and his precious cargo of Mr V, Mr K and two judges would be arriving around 11 o'clock so the telegram said.

At the postal counter Jack received a wonderfully verbose letter of recommendation from a Mr T Edison, verifying the electrification of Torheit and the ratio of knobs and tubes quite satisfactory. It was eight dollars well spent. He put the letter in his pocket, for it would be delicious to whip it out when Quill came to have another poke at his sanity. So far the day was turning out splendidly.

It wasn't until Jack started up the track to Torheit that the day, which had such promise turned to the euphemism of the brown bricks those at Schnider Kiln works were so fond of using. The full enormity of the situation became apparent as he rode his Harley Davidson up the track.

While he had been enjoying beef stew and dumplings the weather had been lashing the countryside.

The track was no more than a muddy slide

down the hill, the steps to the front/back door were undermined, Parsnips collecting tank at the top of the hill was full to overflowing and the whole site was a mess. Torheit stood defiant as chaos reigned.

It was 9:15.

There was nothing to do except call for reinforcements.

Everyone stood on a large shelf of rock and looked at the erosion of the Parson quarter acre. The top soil had slipped down to the creek exposing the rock beneath. It was a dramatic change from undulating grassy knolls.

'I knew Huff Parson put one over me, but for the life of me I couldn't figure out how.' Bill threw a stone at the bedrock which comprised nearly all of the land. 'No bloody topsoil,' he cussed.

'We could get some bushes and...' David Brown said.

'Perhaps we might...' Steinbeck scratched his head.

'Look, whatever we do, we need to do it quick.' Jack took his cap off and began to pull his hair.

'The way I see it,' Hazel said, hands on hips, 'we make the rock a feature. Clear away the remaining dirt. Expose the rock. It looks like Torheit is sitting on an island of rock. I rather like it.' The girl really was something special. Her blood was worth bottling.

There was a mad dash back to the farmhouse and buckets, brooms, shovels and spades were employed to move the remaining dirt.

'I didn't think I'd ever be cleaning rocks,' Steinbeck said to Putney.

'Me neither,' Putney replied sluicing a rock and righting an urn. Meanwhile Swindon and Jack were planting wild flowers under the steps, Bill and Enid were inside checking on things and Hazel was gathering buckets of water. It was a bustle of activity, so much so that the arrival of Noel Braithwaite went un-noticed until he popped up and said,

'How do Mr Renfrew.'

'Arrrhhh.' Jack spun around, a bunch of flowers in his hand.

'What's all this then?'

'Pardon?'

'What's happening?'

'Oh. Last minute tidying, that's all.'

'And that's your last word on it, is it?'

'Definitely Mr Braithwaite.' Jack gave Swindon his flowers and then brushed his hands on his trousers.

'Er, Jack,' Hazel called, 'mother wants you.'

'Right. Excuse me Mr Braithwaite. We have some important visitors coming in less than an hour and well, we are quite busy.'

'I know all about your visitors Mr Renfrew.' That last remark had a bad feeling about it. What Mr Braithwaite knew or thought he knew left Jack feeling quite out of sorts. The press had a way of twisting things, manipulating things and to put it bluntly, lying about things all for the sake of a good story.

'Well, you will be on the spot then, a scoop I think you call it.'

'Oh, I'll be on the spot Mr Renfrew.' Braithwaite took a look at the frenetic activity. 'And I wonder if you happen to know where all the furniture from the Golf Club has gone. I think the Mayor was under the impression he paid for it.'

Jack swallowed—hard. There was nothing for

it, he would need to rely on the press being decent sorts when a fellow was in a pickle.

'Look, Mr Braithwaite, Noel, I'm in a bit of a pickle.'

Noel nodded. He 'ahhed' a few times, he 'hmmmed' a bit and then let out a laugh. 'And you're telling me the Mayor had no idea?'

'Yes.'

Noel let out a guffaw. Jack didn't like the sound of the guffaw. It had the sound of someone who knows something and isn't letting on.

'We'll put it all back, just as soon as the judges have been through.'

'I see.'

'Jack, mother wants you.' Hazel called from the steps.

'Coming.' Jack turned to the reporter, 'The Mayor...he's ignorant, isn't he?'

'Are you asking or telling.' Braithwaite smirked.

'Jack!'

'Right there.' Jack took the steps two at a time and disappeared into the house.

'Is that the reporter?' Enid asked as she looked out of the low window.

'Mr Braithwaite of the City Morning Daily.' Jack answered.

'Braithwaite, he's the fellow who got us into this fine mess. Him and all his 'modern appliances for a modern woman',' Bill said. 'I'd like to ring his neck.

'Get in line Mr Brown,' Jack said.

'Never mind him,' Hazel said, 'look.' She

pointed to the lightshade and the tell-tale signs of a leak in the roof.

Jack wondered if Edgar needed help on the farm in California. He groaned and looked at his watch.

'I told Clutz,' Bill and Enid looked up then looked down. The cross stitch cushion was absorbing all the water without so much as a drop making it to the floor. The word lucky just didn't cover the sheer chance of the incident.

'Just don't move anything.'

'Right you are.'

There was a whistle from outside and they rushed to the low windows to see the Pierce Arrow making its way up the track. David and the gang were retreating up the steps and out of sight.

'I think this is your cue Jack.' Hazel pushed him to the door.

'Can you just look natural Mr and Mrs Brown. Sort of...well...like people.'

'We'll do our best son.'

When VIPs come to town the kerfuffle and commotion can far outweigh the actual importance of the celebrities. Brownsville was a town where notables, dignitaries and bigwigs were thin on the ground. It was inevitable that the Pierce Arrow would attract attention. When those VIPs being conveyed to Torheit were top hatted, grand moustachioed and morning suited people began to talk.

Mayor Wynkoop looked out of his window and caught a glimpse of the passing parade as there was no better word for the cavalcade of traps, horse and buggies, the few automobiles and a dray with the hoi-polloi sitting on hay bales all following the Pierce Arrow as it wended its way through the main street of town.

The Browns, the apprentices, the reporter and Jack watched in amazement as the people kept coming, all churning up the mud, tramping over the cleaned rocks and generally making a picnic of the event.

'What the hay-ho?' Hazel said.

'I think it's turned into an event.' David Brown said and they all looked at Braithwaite.

'I might have said something.' Braithwaite shrugged and grinned and in a neat manoeuvrer of deflection said, 'oh look, there's the Mayor.'

Jack closed his eyes and held his hands over his face while making a noise that came from the pit of despair.

No-one likes to see a grown man cry, so everyone turned and ogled at the notaries, the Mayor and the hoi-polloi.

'Hey there,' Huxley jumped out of the way of a large lady with a large hat and waved to Jack.

Jack waved back and slowly made his way down the steps to certain death. With all these freeloaders traipsing over the ground there was wasn't a snowballs chance in hell the judges would see Torheit in its best light. That light being in splendid isolation on an igneous rock.

'Renfrew,' Huxley slapped his pal on the back.

'How goes it?'

'Oh, you know...' Jack tried to smile, but it came out looking like he'd just had a dose of cod liver oil. 'I still have my hair, although it's a close run thing.'

'And my fellow galley slaves?' Huxley looked around.

'Up there,' Jack pointed to the front/back door.

'Ah,' Huxley looked up the rise then back to the crowds gawking at every sudden move.

'What's all this? You been selling tickets?'

'Something like that.'

The tête-à-tete was interrupted by the Mayor's arrival and the crowd of onlookers being parted like a five cent cut and comb.

'Come on,' Huxley pushed Jack to the Pierce Arrow, 'time to meet and greet.'

'Ah. This is Mr Conrad Popplezig,' Huxley said. 'Judge of the most prestigious Bossart Award for Architectural Excellence.'

'Sir,' Jack nodded and studied the large fellow who looked like he didn't get out from behind the dinner buffet very often. He had a rather large stomach that preceded him everywhere and now sat in an attitude of beneficence, and it was only a huge moustache that gave some proportion to the whole picture.

'Well, pleased to know you,' Mayor Wynkoop busted into the conversation. 'Yes, sir, mighty pleased to know you.'

'Ah,' Jack looked at the Mayor. 'This is Mayor Wynkoop, of Steerforth County.'

'Yes, sir, mighty pleased to know you.' The Mayor pumped Mr Polppezig's hand and beamed. Mr P surreptitiously wiped his hand on his trousers when the Mayor had finished gushing.

'And this,' Huxley turned to a small man with pointy features, 'is Mr William Thrip.'

'Sir,' Jack nodded in deference to the fellow that looked like he lived on not much more than the sliced top off a boiled egg. Thrip turned at his name. He was espousing on the magnificent turn out, the local flora and fauna and how spats are made in China of all places. Mr V had a vacant stare. Mr K had developed a twitch.

A thrip is a small annoying insect that, once attached to something, sucks the life out of it. Mr William Thrip had all of those attributes. He had the knack of talking that sucked your very will to live right out of your bone marrow.

Mr Popplezig at the other end of the spectrum rarely said anything above a grunt. He looked as if the whole world annoyed him and he wished they'd all just go away or stop breathing, or maybe both.

Thrip and Popplezig now had their first sighting of Torheit and Jack tried to read their faces.

'Well, well, well.' Thrip said. 'Well, well, well,' he repeated.

'Hummmph,' Popplezig replied.

Mr Vuoto, Mr Kartoffelkopf.' Jack doffed his cap and opened the automobile door.

Mr Popplezig took the deference and proceeded to step into mud and a cheer erupted from the crowd. He waved—the paper later saying 'regally'—and stepped to a bit of rock lest his spats get spatty.

Mr Thrip alighted and stood to wave to the crowd informing everyone within earshot that he was privy to such a crowd at the opening of the Pennsylvania Station in New York City, that very year. He was just alluding to the buffet put on by the dignitaries when Mr V woke up from his coma, jumped out of the car and careered into Thrip. There was a moment when the crowd held their breath waiting for the splat, but Jack grabbed Thrip and saved the day.

'Just in time lad, just in time.'

'Yes sir.'

Huxley slapped Jack on the back which made Jack let go of Thrip, who by the laws of physics kept up his forward motion and bumped into the Mayor. 'Amazing reflex Renfrew,' Huxley said and they watched as Thrip attached himself to the Mayor and began to suck the will to live from Webster like a two for one special. No-one was about to come to Webster's rescue. Thrip began at the Mayan pyramids and who knows where he would end up by the time they made it to the front/ back door. It didn't take the Mayor long to see he was trapped by his own good manners. How does one extricate oneself from a tedious bore and still stay in the circle of influence. Tricky.

With everyone perched on rocks to save their city shoes it looked like a stalemate. Louis Powell, a photographer who knows which side his bread is buttered came to the rescue and with Braithwaite at his side, the carrot on the stick of publicity got the bigwigs moving, mud or no mud. Louis had them lined up like ducks in no time and as they posed the country folk looked on with amazement and fascination in equal measure. It is not often you see so many ducks in a row. The only duck missing was the Mayor who had slipped away in the melee. Now, of course he could see his mistake.

'Er,' Webster skirted around a young boy with a stick who was poking the mud from a large island of rock, 'excuse me.'

'Huh.' The young lad looked up, 'can you just move, I need to...' Webster pointed to the slab of rock that the other notaries were perched upon. There was nowhere for the lad to go except in the mud. His mother wouldn't like it. He stood his ground.

'Will you get out of my way,' Webster said with as much force as he could muster without garnering attention from the gathering crowd of voters, (for there is always the never ending battle between popularity and authority).

'Move it,' Webster said and shoved the lad into a puddle. He looked over to the island of dignitaries who were smiling for Louis Powell's camera. 'I'm entitled,' the Mayor said. No-one piped up to disprove his whining presumption of entitlement. The word hubris came to mind from a few in the crowd who did crosswords on a regular basis, the other hoi-polloi just curled their top lips and harrumphed.

Mayor Wynkoop reached the plateau of luminaries and muscled his way in looking, or trying to look, awfully important.

'Ah,' Thrip found his mark. 'Did you know the natives of Africa...' The Mayor groaned. There is always a price to pay, and Webster was paying it. He tried to smile for the camera, but as the photograph would later show, the Mayor looked like he had been to Africa and contracted something nasty from the tap water.

Once the media call was out of the way, the group, led by Mr Kartoffelkopf hopped from one stone to the next around the site, to afford a better view, the best view, the view from the other side, and the expansive view. Mr K just about genuflected at every opportunity, it looked like his knees had springs attached. (probably Harrington springs)

'It is good ja?' He hopped onto a rocky outcrop and pointed. The crowd had followed the stepping stone tour and now every pair of eyes looked to Torheit, which was doing its best to shine. Brown bricks that look like, well we all know what they looked like, rarely have the chance to shine.

'It is a work of art no?' Mr V perched precariously on a small rock and smiled at the judges.

'Hmmph.' Mr Popplezig looked at his spats. He squinted at Torheit and if anyone was trying to read his mood, they might have said he had a bad case of wind.

'Tell me, Mr Vol-au-vent,' Mr Thrip said, 'where is the front door?'

'Ah,' Mr Vol-au-vent looked at Mr K.'

'With the linear shapes,' Mr K began when Jack came to the rescue.

'Sir, Torheit is made for the eye to run with the horizontal line. Nothing to disturb the symmetry.'

'Ja.' Mr K nodded. 'Nothing to disturb the symmetry.'

You might have thought that Mr K, and his enormous ego should have been right at home espousing symmetry to the judges of the Bossart Award. And under normal circumstances you'd be correct, but when under pressure for the most prestigious award in one's career, nerves can get the better of anyone, even a narcissist. Mr K drew on his narcissistic reserves and tried to explain the concepts, the modern feel, the 'high falutin'' as someone from the audience said. The gawkers hung on his every word, oohing and ahhhing at every grandiose claim. Once Mr K got his second wind, he threw his arms wide and launched into superlatives with exaggerated hyperbolical fervour.

There is a fine line between obsequious and obnoxious. Mr K had crossed that line and the notaries hadn't got as far as the front/back door.

'Ah.' Mr Thrip squinted at the symmetry and nodded. 'I recollect in the plans there is an entry up there. I once had a night in an igloo and the entry was positioned away from the weather...it was...' and he might have gone on for some time if everyone's attention whipped around when a young lad shouted,

'He did it ma.' The young lad pointed to the Mayor as he straddled a puddle. The mother employed the pointy end of her umbrella and poked the Mayor with an, 'Oi!' Then she took a good long look at Webster Wynkoop and let him know just what she thought of him. The crowd were enthralled. They would have paid good money to watch this kerfuffle. The mother pointed to her son, 'you should be ashamed of yourself. Bullying small children.'

The Mayor put his hands on his hips, 'Madam, I did nothing of the sort. I've never seen your urchin before in my life.'

The audience swivelled their necks as if at a tennis match.

'He pushed me ma.' The lad piped up.

'If I pushed him, he deserved it.' Mayor Wynkoop looked at the V.I.Ps and tried to garner some sympathy. He rolled his eyes at the young boy, 'kids!' It didn't exactly come off as a Buster Keaton, 'oh what an adorable rascal' move.

'Nothing but a hog wallowin' bully.' The mother grabbed her young charge and walked away.

'Who is this fellow?' Mr K asked.

'The Mayor sir,' Jack said. 'Shall we move on?'

And that was how the Mayor was relegated to hog wallowin' status. Unfortunately the hog wallowin' moniker would stick to Webster for some time, and in the future would be blamed for his fall from public office. Such is the hurley-burley of politics.

Just as the party began to rock hop, there was a commotion and they turned to watch the Clutz clan arrive in an automobile truck and Mr Quill arrive by bicycle.

Jack groaned. Quill was the last person he needed to see.

Clutz tooted the crowd out of the way and pulled up next to the Pierce Arrow. Huxley narrowed his eyes at the lackadaisical parking. One vehicle was worth a small fortune, the other looked like it might need a small fortune to be worthy of the title vehicle.

Freelan Quill picked his way across the mud to the group of dignitaries and looked for a familiar face. He spied Jack and narrowed his eyes only to open them wide when he saw Braithwaite.

'Still chasing immortality Quill.' Braithwaite asked.

'Some of us have work to do Mr Braithwaite.' Quill was about to say more, when Mr Clutz yelled,

'Hey,' Vern waved at the dignitaries and came bounding over with his three sons in tow.

'Um. This is the builder sir.' Jack made the introductions.

'Hummmmphf.'

'Well, well, well.'

'This here is Skeet, Woodruff and Winslow.' Vern went to spit, but the evil eye from Jack made him reconsider. 'We reckon this here apple crate of yours is the darndest thing.'

'Apple crate?' Mr Thrip asked.

'We reckon it looks like an apple crate,' Winslow said.

'Apple crate,' Skeet echoed and nodded.

Everyone, from the judges, Mr V, Mr K and the hoi-polloi took a good long look at Torheit. It was one of those silent revelations. Sort of like when you finally realise your favourite uncle is totally bonkers when you thought he was just a jolly joker all these years.

'It *does* looks like an apple crate,' someone in the crowd said.

'So it does.' The nomenclature was repeated and flew around the crowd.

Braithwaite wrote it down. He could envisage the headline. SHE'LL BE APPLES! Louis took a photo.

'Apfelkiste?' Mr Kartoffelkopf said a little confused.

'Apfelkiste.' Jack repeated. 'It has a nice ring to it.' They looked at the building. 'Mr Kartoffelkopf?'

'Ja, Apfelkiste.' It might just be a literal translation to German of apple crate, but much like a hog wallowin' bully, once a name fits, it's hard to call it anything else.

'Ah, what a fitting name for a modern utilitarian, structure with function and form. I do recall in Berlin I had the opportunity...' Thrip got hold of Skeet and began to suck the life from the witless fellow.

Jack heard the two words from the bible of Architecture, 'function and form', and took the first steps to a promising career. He looked at the gathered group of worthies, 'shall we?'

The big wigs hopped from igneous rock to igneous rock to arrive at the steps, then made the climb to the front/back door leaving the gawkers behind.

CHAPTER 25

Enid and Bill stood to attention as the judges trooped inside followed by their entourage, the Mayor and Quill bringing up the rear. If gall and audacity were being handed out like toffee apples, Quill and Wynkoop might have taken two each. Jack sucked in his lips and tried his hand at a withering stare at the pair. It didn't work as they sauntered into the house as if they couldn't imagine being anywhere else.

'Renfrew,' Quill said.

'Quill,' Jack replied trying not to curl his top lip.

Enid, being unaccustomed to V.I.Ps, went a little silly. She curtseyed and giggled and adjusted her best hat.

'Enid, behave,' Bill jabbed her in the ribs with his elbow.

'Mother,' Hazel grabbed her mother's arm. The poor woman was all a tizz. She'd never met a man with spats and a top hat before.

'Mr Popplezig, Mr Thrip,' Jack muscled his way to the receiving line, 'This is Mr and Mrs Brown.'

'Pleased to meet you,' Bill held out his hand.

'Oooo. Pleasure I'm sure,' Enid curtseyed again.

The judges eyed the Browns. Mr Popplezig reluctantly took the hand.

'Nice day for it,' Bill said.

'Hummmmphf.'

'Did you know the chances of...' Thrip began which prompted a quick exodus into the spacious lounge room.

'This here is the fire place,' Bill said and pointed to the large rock with an even larger chimney flue over it.

Mr K stood to one side and patted the rock lovingly while looking at Popplezig with an expression bordering on sycophantic.

'Humphf.' Mr P glanced around the room and all the modern furniture which was nowhere near the fire. If you wanted to warm your footsies you'd need to have extra-long legs.

When Mr P did speak it wasn't what Mr K wanted to hear. 'Not exactly functional is it?'

After locating where the cat had put his tongue, Mr K took umbrage.

'What?

'Functional.' Mr Popplezig enunciated for Mr K.

Jack popped up, 'Form over function, sir.'

'Ja. Form over Function.'

'We used dynamite,' Bill said. 'Couldn't budge the bugger.'

'Bill!'

' KaBOOM!' Bill spread his hands wide and

everyone jumped.

'Dynamite eh? When I was in South Africa, the dynamite employed...' Thrip said while everyone bolted to the windows out of his line of sight.

Mr V hovered. This was his time to shine. He hopped from one foot to another and acted like a toddler who needs to go potty.

'You see the lines, no?' He pointed to the two seater that no-one dare sit on. 'It is here we make the man in our own image, no.'

No, thought Hazel. If Mr V had a man in mind, then that poor unfortunate wouldn't have a spine to speak of by the end of the day. Chairs were supposed to be a welcome relief, not something that required a neck brace for a week afterwards.

'Oh, this is rather nice,' Mr Thrip went to pick up the cross-stich cushion.

'NO!' Hazel and Jack threw themselves at the man and tackled him to the occasional table, then threw him down on the two seater, which promptly threw him to the ground. It all happened so fast, no-one was quite sure who did what to whom.

Thrip bounded up and took the Marquess of Queensbury rules boxing stance.

'Eh?' Popplezig turned at the commotion and swiped a standard lamp with his girth. Hazel caught it just in time.

'Nice catch,' Huxley said.

'Yes, isn't she,' Jack said looking with admiration at the woman who's blood he'd like to bottle. 'Salt of the earth if you ask me.'

Hazel blushed.

'You know,' Mayor Wynkoop frowned and pointed, 'I think I bought the very same chair, for my golf clubhouse.'

'Really?' Jack looked at Hazel who was still holding the lamp.

'Then you have excellent taste, Mayor Wynkoop.' The Mayor puffed out his chest.

'No, it is not possible. No,' Mr V said knowing he had only designed one cantilever torture devise and that was for Torheit/Apfelkiste.

Jack looked at Bill. It was all coming undone, right before their eyes. Bill shrugged and shoved his hands in his pockets and had a think. It needed to be quick.

'Have ya seen my gentlemen's bathroom?' he announced.

'Oh, you must see the gentlemen's bathroom,' Hazel said.

'Yes, the gentlemen's bathroom is really something,' Jack added.

'Top class,' Huxley joined in ushering the dignitaries down the hall. 'I hear they have hot and cold running water.'

'Sir?' Jack stepped back for Mr V and Mr K.

'Mayor,' Hazel shooed the stragglers, Quill the last to go.

'Mrs Brown,' Jack saw Enid locked into position at the fireplace, a blank look on her face. The hullabaloo all a bit too much.

'Mother?' Hazel put down the lamp and rubbed her mother's back.

'Eh?'

'Afternoon tea mother. Lots and lots of afternoon tea.'

'Oh.' Enid snapped to attention. If there was one thing she excelled at, it was food.

'That's it. Afternoon tea. A brilliant idea,' Jack

said, so pleased with the suggestion he grabbed Hazel and whirled her around, then planted a kiss where a kiss ought to go.'

'Jack,' Hazel adjusted her hair and skirt.

'You are just the most amazing woman.'

'Am I?'

'Hazel,' Enid came to her senses. She took off her best hat and said, 'I need help.'

'Right.' Hazel trotted after her mother, then turned and winked at Jack.

'Nice work if you can get it,' Huxley said.

'Yes, very nice,' Jack replied.

When you get seven gentlemen in a gentlemen's bathroom there isn't much room for much else. Bill's little black book came out and he thumbed through the pages. He pointed out the various features of his gentlemen's bathroom, noting the price, the competition and the bonus of 10% off—in the case of Hutton's Hot Water System.

The men admired the Hutton hot water system. They marvelled at the taps from McCreedy's Porcelain Emporium and then their eyes turned to the Gutfeldt weight reducing belt.

'Ah.' Bill stepped up to the mark. If there is one thing a man who reads the catalogue religiously knows about, it is the advertised benefits of what is on offer. Bill could recite the said benefits of the Munroe weed puller, the Fuller cattle feeder with easy to move axles and now the Gutfeldt weight reducing belt. The salesmen had espoused the virtues, the benefits and the wonderful rewards of health into old age to Bill. Bill remembered it all.

His audience listened enraptured by the spiel. Bill hypnotised them with vital statistics, he delighted them with the promise of health and vitality and enthralled them with a demonstration.

'electricityyyyyyyyyyyyyyyyyy,'

Bill said as he vibrated his way to vigour and verve.

Now you might think that seeing a farmer whose waist had disappeared sometime in the late 1880's because his wife thought the way to a man's heart is through his stomach, might not be such an alluring sight. There was none of that at all. It wasn't long before all the men were stripped to their trousers and shirts lining up to have a go.

'marvellllllllloussssssssssssssss,'   Mayor Wynkoop said.

'myyyyyyy wordddddddddd,' Quill pulsated.

'Wwwwoooonnnnnnnddddderrrrffffffuuuuuuuullll,' Mr Thrip jiggled—not that he had much to jiggle.

Mr V could only get out a 'nnnnnnnnoooooooo.' And predictably Mr K was stuck with 'jjjjjjjjjjjjjjjjaaaaaaaa.'

Then, as they all watched, Mr Popplezig took his turn.

If the Gutfeldt was going to prove its worth, here was the challenge.

Mr P stepped up to the machine. The Gutfeldt took a deep breath and after all the straps and contraptions were adjusted, got to work. And work it did, to its most glorious health benefits and beyond. Mr P jiggled. He wriggled. He waggled and a smile crept across his face.

'Simplyyyyyy   splennnnnndidddd.'   Mr   P

beamed. The arresting sight of a very large fellow having the jiggle jiggled out of him is kinda mesmerizing. Mr P's audience watched transfixed as the Gutfeldt worked its magic, for it was magic— as Mr P's countenance took on a broad grin rather than a gruff annoyance as if one had dressed in a hurry and put ones underpants on back to front.

'It's electricity,' Bill said. 'Really quite remarkable stuff. It's very, very handy.' The crowd nodded in acceptance of a universal truth.

Eventually the men emerged from the bathroom full of good cheer, and overflowing with the rosy glow of health giving benefits dispensed by Gutfeldt and his weight reducing belt.

Huxley had rounded up the apprentices and they had practically raided the Brown's farm larder. Now the lads ushered the V.I.Ps to the kitchen in what Jack thought a last ditch effort to impress. He need not have tried too hard—Gutfeldt had done the hard work for him.

Enid stood—Queen of the kitchen. The large dining table, the only thing that had not been replaced waited, groaning under the weight of good ol' home cooking. Swindon licked his lips and almost swooned at the food.

'Gentlemen,' Enid said, 'sit.'

Gutfeldt might have the market in weight reducing, but he couldn't hold a candle to Enid's weight increasing home cooking.

Mr Popplezig's eyes popped. Mr V and Mr K pulled up their chairs so quick you might think they were brought up in an orphanage. The Mayor and

Quill sat down and positioned their napkin like old hands.

'Tea anyone?' Hazel held the teapot aloft.

To describe the afternoon tea as a success would be a gross understatement. Cakes, sponges, cookies, tarts, scones with jam and gallons of cream all went around the table and back again.

Mr Thrip ate more than the top off a boiled egg. Thankfully he had been brought up with manners and didn't utter a word while his mouth was full. He indulged himself on jam tarts, Bakewell tarts, and slices of sponge cake with cream filling.

Popplezig knew how to pack away a good afternoon tea when it was presented. He tried everything—some twice.

Perhaps Enid's mother had been right all along when she dispensed some marital advice to her daughter all those years ago.

'Enid, the way to a man's heart is through his stomach.' Enid had been applying that advice ever since.

'You think we will make it work?' Hazel sidled up to Jack.

'I do.' Jack said, sliding his hand into hers.

'I do too,' Hazel said clasping his hand tight, quite aware of the double entendre.

'Alright you two?' Huxley slid up to the pair.

'Yes thanks,' Jack said, adding 'FABRUM ESSE SUAE QUEMQUE.'

'Ah,' Hazel beamed at Jack. 'Each man the architect of his own fate.'

'Exactly,' Roman said and helped himself to a raspberry tart.

'Looks like you still have a head of hair.' Swindon said between bites of cherry pie.

'I really could get accustomed to the country you know,' Steinbeck said to Putney.

'Salt of the earth eh?' Putney replied and took a scone.

'All it takes is a leap of faith,' Mr Thrip was saying.

'All it takes is a bit of money,' Bill replied.

'Art has no price,' Mr Otto Kartoffelkopf said.

'And good ol' American knowhow,' Mr Popplezig said.

'And three sticks of dynamite,' Bill added.

'And you have an icon.' Jack offered.

'And a gentlemen's bathroom with the best view in the house.' Bill grinned.

'And a Hoover,' Enid smiled.

There was a rousing cheer from the table as Mr K said, 'ja,' to a second helping of all American apple pie—which was quite fitting for a home called Apfelkiste.

The certificate hung in the kitchen.

"APFELKISTE"

BOSSART AWARD
FOR ARCHITECTURAL
EXCELLENCE

And underneath someone had added.

The best apple pie
this side of the Mason Dixon line.

And a new cross stitch was hung over the fire
place.

*The way to a man's heart
is through his stomach.*

All my books and social media are available from this link

www.linktr.ee/hettieashwin

I'm also loitering on-line in the usual places. Amazon, B & Noble, Apple, Goodreads et al.

Reviews help authors enormously.

If you want to leave a review it would be most welcome
Thanks
Hettie.

p.s. I have a newsletter which will keep you up to date on all my writings etc. There is a free novella waiting for you when you sign up.
newsletter signup
http://eepurl.com/hbbKpv